KILL *the* DRAGON

RECLAIMING YOUR LIFE FROM THE DARK SIDE OF RELIGION

GUNTER AKRIDGE

HIGHER PERSPECTIVES
PRESS

Kill the Dragon

Copyright © 2023 Gunter Akridge

Higher Perspectives Press

Cover and Interior Layout by Matt M Higgins, Doxology Creative

Edited by Hope Myers

Author Photograph by Christian Jay, Three Lines Creative

ISBN: 979-8-218-21897-3 (Paperback)
ISBN: 979-8-218-24876-5 (Hardback)
ISBN: 979-8-218-21898-0 (eBook)
ISBN: 979-8-218-24437-8 (Audio)

Printed in the United States of America

For additional information, visit www.killthedragonbook.com.

ENDORSEMENTS

"Kill the Dragon is a personal journey of a man who carries a deep desire to see people move beyond realities that limit, constrain and deter you from living freely in all that you were designed to be. Let today be the day you move into a space you long for and desire to be: which is to be fully alive."

—
Eric Johnson
Pastor, Author, Communicator | Studio Church, Greenville, SC

"Jesus is leading the church where religion, offense, and control cannot go. Only love and truth, and lots of it. This is the heart and soul of Kill the Dragon. Unpacking his own story, Gunter Akridge offers the church a brilliant vision to fight against the religious mindsets and minefields so deeply embedded in the Christian culture. I'm convinced this conversation matters more than ever. Kill the Dragon not only exposes the lies and trappings of the religious spirit, but challenges the church to face the dragon, head on. In our day of theological drift, political polarization, sexual confusion, and spiritual trauma, not to mention one million people leaving the church in the US yearly, we need a better way. This book is a hope-filled journey from fearful, reactive and suspicious religion into powerful, fearless and spirit-drenched renewal ~ the kind the world longs for. A war cry for leaders, parents and disciples ready to name, confront and kill the religious spirit in the church, let alone in our lives, homes and families. For such a time as this."

—
Nate Edwardson
Pastor | Stirring Church, Redding, CA

"Kill The Dragon is both a relieving and powerful read. Gunter has shared finally his wisdom on slaying the legalistic and often cruel side of religion, one that we often reference, but one that we may not be able to break down the way this author has. From his own personal experiences, as well as his hermeneutical analysis to back and fight for the true meaning of freedom within the gospel, you're led on a finer understanding of how to tackle and finally slay the dragon of the dark side of religion. A must read for this current age. By the end of the book, you find yourself thinking 'with an educational approach like this, we have hope for the church after all.'"

—
Carrie Lloyd
Journalist and Author of The Noble Renaissance

"Reading this book, I could see Gunter's passionate expressions and hear the compassion in his voice. It takes courage to write a book that shines a light into the murky shadows of religion. Gunter identifies the problem, then offers us all the opportunity to seek the wisdom of the Holy Spirit, the love of Father God and the lordship of Jesus Christ. Light always brings awareness and choice. Adeptly Gunter gives the reader information gleaned from experience, built on a foundation of the Word of God and historical context. The choice remains ours to make. Once the problem is identified, then we have practical applications to help us on our own journey. The journey Gunter continues to travel. Gunter Akridge is curious and bold with a genuine humility. It's an interesting character mix. He will seek first the Word of God and the guidance of Holy Spirit, then he will seek the wisdom of counsel. He is a wise leader willing to take risks. Gunter willingly receives wise counsel and gives it.

My endorsement of this book is an endorsement of Gunter. He lives his life opposite of one who is marked by the influence of the religious spirit. Having walked with him through many seasons of ministry and family life, he is a genuine disciple, filled with the love of God and obedient."

—
Theresa Harris
Former Associate Pastor | Bridgeway Church, Greenville, SC

TABLE OF CONTENTS

Foreword   9

ONE
Into the Dragon's Lair   13

TWO
Chapter Two: Law Over Love   31

THREE
Belief Over Experience   43

FOUR
Tradition Over Truth   53

FIVE
Avoidance Over Influence   65

SIX
Doctrine Over Devotion   77

SEVEN
Control Over Trust   89

EIGHT
Offense Over Humility   103

NINE
Dragon Legends   113

TEN
Destructive Intent   125

ELEVEN
Dragon Speech   137

TWELVE
Confronting the Dragon   145

THIRTEEN
Expanding Horizons   163

FOURTEEN
A Land With No Dragons   173

Acknowledgments   185

DEDICATION

This book is dedicated to the people of The Dwelling Church.
It has been the honor of my life to kill dragons with you.

Foreword

What you're about to read is a love story. Gunter's love for the Church is evident on every page. In a culture that's grown far too comfortable with criticism, Gunter doesn't just call out the Church for her flaws; he calls her up. Hard topics are addressed here, but not without tender care and affection for God's people. Gunter never writes from frustration. He doesn't have an axe to grind or a bone to pick. Rather, he has caught a glimpse of the power and freedom of slaying this fire-breathing dragon that scorches the Church time and time again.

As Jesus walked with his disciples, he warned them not to partake in the "leaven of the Pharisees," but sadly, that very same yeast continues getting worked into the bread that we, the Church, serve to this day. It grows and spreads quickly through every batch of dough it touches. When the Israelites prepared for Passover, God instructed them to clean every speck of yeast out of their homes. It's time to go through all the cupboards and pantries and clean house.

Before you dig in, you should know that this isn't a book about "them." Gunter loves the Church far too much to write a book aimed outward. Rather, this is a book about us. Even more so, this is a book about you and me. Gunter isn't here to equip you with hand grenades to lob at others but rather a sword and shield to defend yourself against the devil himself. As you read, invite the Holy Spirit to nudge your heart with conviction and expect him to challenge you in the best way possible. There are tools here to help you examine your heart for any places that have become contaminated by a religious spirit, a mindset of legalism, and a heart lacking in God's unconditional love.

Ultimately, this love story is here to equip you to love better. Jesus is coming back for a pure and spotless Bride. Our love for him and for each other must be pure and holy, just like he is. The enemy would love nothing more than to rob Jesus of the kind of love he deserves, but in this hour, God is purifying his Church to make her ready for the Bridegroom. Allow the Lord to challenge your thinking as you read, and you will discover that the love he desires from you comes directly from the love he's pouring into you. It is the love of Jesus that slays the dragon. My prayer for you as you read is that empty, religious mindsets would get stripped away as you encounter the rich expanse of God's love.

—
Wes Pickering
Speaker, Worship Leader, and Author of *Monuments of Grace: Living a Life Laid Down in Authentic Worship* and *Psalm 119: God's Key to Unlock Scripture*

CHAPTER ONE

Into the Dragon's Lair

I love to read. But before college, I rarely finished books, especially novels. I started plenty of them, but the next exciting thing always enticed my attention away. ADHD is real. So, if you're in that boat, I get you!

The dreamer in me was apt to travel to other worlds, leaving me clueless about what my eyes mindlessly scanned over while I was momentarily "absent." Then I'd go back and read it. If I wasn't interested, books just closed, never to be opened again.

But that all changed one day when I went to the mall with my parents as a pre-teen. On that particular day, I walked into a bookstore and picked up the thickest novel I'd ever seen. Okay, maybe I'd seen thicker ones, but I never would have thought twice about actually reading them.

This book was paperback with a hunter green cover that read, The Hobbit by J.R.R. Tolkien. After seeing the old animated film version, I knew the basic story. I've got to admit; it was one of my favorites as a kid (if you haven't seen that one, do yourself a favor and immerse yourself in the world of random 1980s Saturday morning cable television.)

Head down with my nose in that book, accompanied, I'm sure, by a Whitney Houston hit, I shuffled through department stores, past the faceless mannequins donned in their denim and oversized flannel. I weaved through the masses, standing in line at the food court with the fragrances of stir-fry, pizza, and cinnamon rolls wafting in the air. Occasionally, I looked up just long enough to ensure I wouldn't run into anything and was still on my mother's heels as we made our way through the crowds.

This story had my attention. The thrill of adventure. The depth of the characters. A classic, and rightfully so. I was glued to it for weeks. It made its mark on me, as all good literature does.

I took a personality test once and received the classification of "peacemaker." I'm not really into conflict. I love peace and comfort. But there's also a wild dreamer in me with a thirst for adventure. I'm a paradox, I guess. But I found a kindred spirit in the little hobbit, Bilbo Baggins. He loved the comfort of home but found himself very much suited for danger and great exploits. This particular journey that Bilbo found himself dragged into revealed his true self. The peril uncovered his hidden courage and character.

The narrative follows Bilbo's journey with a company of dwarves determined to reclaim a long-hidden treasure in the heart of the mountain. This stolen inheritance, rightfully their own, had been in the possession of a great dragon for 171 years. And now, Bilbo, acting as the hired burglar for the dwarves, approaches the lair of the dragon. As he makes his way down the tunnel into the very belly of fear itself, he can hear the rumble of a giant beast. With every step, the heat intensifies; and so does his hesitation. In a moment of fear, paralyzed by the unknown, he stops. To continue on this quest would require a kind of bravery he has never known.

Over time, and with some history behind me, I still identify with this incredible story. It has given language to a spiritual journey of my own, a trip I invite you to take with me in the following pages. They contain a message dear to my heart and flow from a personal experience that has changed how I view my identity as a child of God and a disciple of Jesus.

I have faced a dragon head-on, and it has been the fight of my life. This "dragon" is the religious spirit. I've chosen to refer to the religious spirit as a dragon because there is no better description to communicate the insidious nature of this dangerous mindset. That's what this dragon of the religious spirit is: a mindset. And it's not a man-made idea at all. The religious mindset is demonic in origin and bent on keeping the Church powerless, passionless, fearful, and distracted. This dragon is powerful, cunning, and has an insatiable desire for treasure, namely a treasure that doesn't belong to him — the children of God. He is a smooth-talking hoarder of power and knowledge hidden within the deep recesses of history and the heart of the Church. He's utterly unrecognizable unless you know what you're looking for. His fiery breath, a zealous blaze, has engulfed individuals and societies, captivating them with its doctrine, rituals, and dogmas. He fiercely defends long-held beliefs and traditions with threats of destruction. This dragon must not be ignored. No. It must be awakened, confronted, and killed if we are going to take the mountains God has promised us.

The heartache I've experienced over the spiritual abuse perpetrated in the name of God comes fresh to my senses, and if I'm honest, righteous anger wells up inside of me. I get angry at what religion did to me personally, and I get angry at how religion has robbed so many of their God-given identity and purpose.

You can identify with how I feel. Perhaps you have seen Jesus misrepresented by religion. Maybe you have been influenced by this dragon and, like me, have been used as his puppet to bring spiritual harm to people. But I want to encourage you: there is a new way to think. There is a new way of life that Jesus is inviting us into, and it has no scent of religion at all.

I want to be clear at the start. This book doesn't attack any person or church, or organized religion. I have no axes to grind. No human being or church structure is the target of any indignation here. However, there is a clear enemy named within these pages. Jesus called him the father of lies (John 8:44). In this book, I want to expose the lies of this enemy and reveal the beautiful truths that the religious spirit has overshadowed.

I'm thrilled you are coming along for this adventure. But be prepared for a battle. You'll need your armor because we'll be waking up some sleeping dragons and running the sword of the Spirit (the Word of God) into the heart of the beast that has kept us in bondage. So, suit up, dragon slayer! Let's put some lies to rest for good.

As the appointed time for His crucifixion and death drew near, Jesus set out for Jerusalem to accomplish His reason for coming to earth. The gospel writer, Luke, gives us insight into an intriguing conversation between Jesus and His disciples:

> As the time approached for Him to be taken up to Heaven, Jesus resolutely set out for Jerusalem. And He sent messengers on ahead, who went into a Samaritan village to get things ready for Him; but the people there did not welcome Him, because He was heading for Jerusalem. When the disciples James and John saw this, they asked, "Lord, do you want us to call fire down from heaven to destroy them?" But Jesus turned and rebuked them.
>
> LUKE 9:51-55 NIV

Some manuscripts include this clarification: "And He said, 'You do not know what kind of spirit you are of. For the Son of Man did not come to destroy the lives of men, but to save them.'" (Luke 9:55-56 NKJV) First, let's let the fact that Jesus rebukes his disciples sit with us for a moment. Jesus often corrects them in love. But hear the sternness in His tone here. There is something in what they are suggesting that really gets off with Jesus. He doesn't like it one bit and doesn't hesitate to bring a clarifying statement to the root of their question.

Second, I want you to consider the context of the disciples' request. These guys had been sent out by Jesus earlier in the chapter with the charge to tell everyone about the Kingdom of God and to heal the sick and cast out demons (Luke 9:1-2). So I would imagine that when they first went out, they were skeptical as to whether or not they could actually do what they had watched Jesus do, a little nervous, perhaps.

But now, when they return, there is no question. They've seen demons flee and sick people healed because of their prayers. They're pumped!

They're ready to take on Hell itself! These guys got a glimpse into the raw power of God, and this time it wasn't just observation. They set people free from demonic torment and sickness. Imagine the thrill they must have felt!

With this fresh sense of identity and outrageous faith, they make a shocking request of Jesus:

"Lord, do you want us to call fire down from Heaven to destroy them?"

The hubris is revolting. Their request reeks of self-righteous pride. But it's deeper than that. The disciples ask Jesus's permission to punish the people in this village, to make them suffer, all because they won't roll out the red carpet for them.

Let it sink in.

"Can you believe these people?! How dare they reject us! They deserve to burn!"

The most confusing thing is that they expected Jesus to respond positively to this!

"Sure, boys! Let's torch 'em!" was what I imagine they were waiting to hear.

Instead, with a grieving heart and holy indignation, Jesus says something completely unexpected and very revealing, not just about their heart and motivation, but also about His own: "You do not know what kind of spirit you are of. For the Son of Man did not come to destroy the lives of men, but to save them" (Luke 9:55).

Wow. How could the disciples ask something like this? How could they not have known that Jesus would respond this way? Jesus had not come to destroy people but to rescue them. It seems like a no-brainer to us. But slow down. They may have had good reason to think this way. After all, they knew what happened to Sodom and Gomorrah in their Torah. Fire rained down from Heaven in judgment on the people there. Why not here and now? What was different with this village?

Their thinking was informed by a scriptural principle concerning the judgment of God upon people who were disobedient and rejecting Him.

It's true that the judgment of God will ultimately deal with humanity's rebellion and rejection of His love and salvation. But his judgment is expressed within the context of His fierce love for humanity:

> The Lord passed before him and proclaimed, "The Lord, the Lord, a God merciful and gracious, slow to anger, and abounding in steadfast love and faithfulness, keeping steadfast love for thousands, forgiving iniquity and transgression and sin, but who will by no means clear the guilty, visiting the iniquity of the fathers on the children and the children's children, to the third and the fourth generation.
>
> EXODUS 34:6-7 ESV

The prophet Joel echoes the relenting mercy of God:

> And rend your hearts and not your garments. Return to the Lord your God, for He is gracious and merciful, slow to anger, and abounding in steadfast love; and He relents over disaster.
>
> JOEL 2:13 ESV

The boys had the principles right, but they needed to catch up on the heart of the matter. Instead, they majored in one aspect of God's nature while completely ignoring the rest of who He is. This, my friends, is the heart of the religious spirit. The lie contains enough truth to make you think it's true. Perversion is never cut and dry or black and white. At its heart, it's a twisting of something true and right into something ugly and sinister in its application. This is how the dragon of religion is so deceptive. It is possible to be right and wrong at the same time.

Let's reread Jesus's rebuke: "You do not know what kind of spirit you are of. For the Son of Man did not come to destroy the lives of men, but to save them" (Luke 9:55). "You do not know...." I want to lean into this thought for a moment. The disciples clearly didn't understand the gravity of the statement they were making nor how distant it was from the true heart of God for people. But, again, how could they not know? I want to pose a question to you. If it is possible for Jesus' friends, who knew Him in person, followed Him, and watched His every move, to miss the point entirely, don't you think we could be mistaken about some things, too?

We would all agree that we probably don't have a handle on truth completely, so what if we invited the Holy Spirit to reveal those things to us as we take this journey together? An old preacher once said, "The ignorant don't know they're ignorant."

I have resembled that remark more than I like to admit. But I'm human, just like you are. And we both need the grace of Jesus to see clearly, understand the Father's heart, and live accordingly. If you would embrace humility with me and open your mind and heart to the possibility of being wrong, pray this prayer under your breath to Jesus right now:

> *Heavenly Father, I want to know you. I want my life to reflect the beauty of Jesus in every way. I invite Your Holy Spirit to illuminate any misconceptions or errors in my thinking concerning who You are. I invite You to change my mind. Help me to see where religion has blinded me and open my spiritual eyes to see how You see me and others. In Jesus' name, amen.*

Our behavior is determined by how we think. Even our desires — the things we want — find their root in our thinking. That's why the Bible says, "As a man thinks, so is he" (Proverbs 23:7). Think about the outworking of that truth. The person you currently are is a result of your thinking. Moreover, the person you will become is tied to your thought life. The process of sanctification itself is primarily a work that takes place in our minds. It really does matter how you think. Not only can we change how we think, but how we think can also change us. In

Paul's letter to the Romans, he says:

> Do not conform to the pattern of this world, but be transformed by the renewing of your mind. Then you will be able to test and approve what God's will is — his good, pleasing and perfect will.
>
> ROMANS 12:2 NIV

I'm about to say something that might change your whole way of thinking. It did for me. Are you ready? Not every thought you have is your own.

I'm not talking about originality here. I'm referring to something more profound at the core of our being. Let me explain. We are not human beings having a spiritual experience. We are spiritual beings having a human experience. And God the Father made us to live with a spiritual reality always in view.

As spiritual beings, we have spiritual abilities. Every human does. We're hardwired for the spiritual realm. Therefore, we don't just naturally perceive our surroundings. Have you ever entered a room and suddenly felt a sense of fear within you? How about that feeling you get when you're around someone and something feels off?

We've all been there. You know when someone has that "creeper vibe"! Call it intuition or call it a spiritual sense. It's undeniable. We are inundated with signals like these every day. So much of our inner dialogue, or self-talk, is just our minds processing information. But a significant portion of what we talk to ourselves about is spiritual, whether we realize it or not.

While much of our thought life is benign, some thoughts can carry much more significance, especially if what we think is false. There are things we believe that we totally believe are the truth, but the reality is: they're not. We just think they are.

We'll call this an untruth. An untruth willfully communicated to someone has another name — a lie. If we are engaged in a spiritual battle, and our enemy is called the "father of lies," it is only reasonable to assume that our enemy's main tactic in this war is to lie to us. And when we hear a lie enough, we begin to believe it, and then it starts to produce more lies, and before we know it, we're surrounded by a fortress of untruths that we built ourselves in partnership with the enemy.

This fortress is what the Bible calls a stronghold.

You have undoubtedly seen medieval-style castles in movies with an invading army bombarding the castle's walls with huge boulders flying from their catapults. These medieval fortresses were built with one goal in mind — to keep the enemy out. They were seemingly impenetrable. The first obstacle the enemy would have to cross was the watery moat before scaling or breaching the "curtain wall," the outer wall of the fortress. If the marauders got over the wall, they still had the formidable "keep" to surmount. The "keep" was located in the middle of the fortress and was the last line of defense in an attack. It was the final resort in the event of a siege. In medieval castles, the keep walls could be anywhere from eight to twelve feet thick, sometimes more.

Does this paint a picture for you about how significant strongholds of the mind can be? Think of it this way. Every thought you have is building a fortress around you. Thoughts based on truth create an impenetrable barrier that the enemy cannot breach. But it is also possible that lies we believe can surround us, trap us, and insulate us to truth, keeping us from freedom.

The Apostle Paul tells us what to do with these thoughts that are not from God: "We demolish arguments and every pretension that sets itself up against the knowledge of God, and we take captive every thought to make it obedient to Christ" (2 Corinthians 10:5). Arresting thoughts require us to discern truth from lies, and that takes knowing the truth really well. That truth is found in the Word of God. Letting the "Word of Christ richly dwell within you" (Colossians 3:16) is the key to winning the war over your mind. Don't be ignorant of his schemes (2 Corinthians 2:11). That's what the enemy wants more than anything else, that we would be utterly unaware of what we're thinking.

The dragon of the religious spirit has lied to us, sleeping on an inheritance that rightfully belongs to God's kids. He has been there so long we don't even know he's there. Many false mindsets were built by lies we didn't even realize we were believing. They might have been religious mindsets passed down to us by our parents, churches, or the people who modeled religious life for us. And the sobering thing is, just like the disciples who wanted to call down fire, we have been entirely unaware of it.

You might be saying, "Wait a minute, Gunter. Where is this in the Bible?" Well, let's take a look together.

> The god of this age has blinded the minds of unbelievers, so that they cannot see the light of the gospel that displays the glory of Christ, who is the image of God.
>
> 2 CORINTHIANS 4:4 NIV

> Now this I say and testify in the Lord, that you must no longer walk as the Gentiles do, in the futility of their minds. They are darkened in their understanding, alienated from the life of God because of the ignorance that is in them, due to their hardness of heart. They have become callous and have given themselves up to sensuality, greedy to practice every kind of impurity. But that is not the way you learned Christ!—assuming that you have heard about him and were taught in him, as the truth is in Jesus, to put off your old self, which belongs to your former manner of life and is corrupt through deceitful desires, and to be renewed in the spirit of your minds, and to put on the new

self, created after the likeness of God in true righteousness and holiness.

EPHESIANS 4:17-24 ESV

These verses primarily refer to unbelievers, and the enemy's role in keeping them blinded and bound to the gospel's truth. But scripture also speaks to the fact that the enemy can deceive believers. Paul warned the Church at Galatia about the subtle tactics of Satan among them:

O foolish Galatians! Who has bewitched you? It was before your eyes that Jesus Christ was publicly portrayed as crucified. Let me ask you only this: Did you receive the Spirit by works of the law or by hearing with faith? Are you so foolish? Having begun by the Spirit, are you now being perfected by the flesh?

GALATIANS 3:1 ESV

Here, Paul was referring to the religious mindset that had begun to blind believers in the Galatian Church. As a result, they were departing from true grace and trying to accomplish the Christian life by their own power and practice. (This is a genuine mark of the religious spirit in operation, but I'll get to that soon.)

Paul had a similar warning for the Corinthians: "But I am afraid that as the serpent deceived Eve by his cunning, your thoughts will be led astray from a sincere and pure devotion to Christ" (2 Corinthians 11:3). A follower of Jesus can be deceived and completely unaware. And that, my friends, is the insidious nature of deception. When you are deceived, you don't know it.

If you're a child of the 80s, you probably remember the Transformers cartoon on television. I know. That's two Saturday morning cartoon references. I'm an overgrown kid. Anyway, remember the lines to the opening theme song? "Transformers! More than meets the eye!" That's so true of the spirit of religion. It may not be what you think it is. The disciples didn't know they had been influenced by a spirit that was not the Holy Spirit. The religious leaders of Jesus' day were deceived, and Jesus knew it. My favorite passages are the exchanges between Him and the religious crowd. They reveal so much about the nature of religious deception.

Here's a beautiful example of religious ignorance for your reading pleasure:

> So Jesus said to the Jews who had believed him, "If you abide in my word, you are truly my disciples, and you will know the truth, and the truth will set you free." They answered him, "We are offspring of Abraham and have never been enslaved to anyone. How is it that you say, 'You will become free'?"
>
> JOHN 8:30-33 ESV

Did you catch that? "We have never been enslaved to anyone." So, here's the crazy thing. Their Jewish ancestors had indeed been slaves despite their refusal to see it. I mean, a large chunk of Jewish history is the story of God's redemptive love for His people, releasing them from bondage repeatedly. First, they were slaves for 400 years in Egypt, then it was the Babylonian Exile around the year 586 BC, and after that, the Persian Empire ruled over them. At the moment they said this to Jesus, the Jews were under Roman occupation in their homeland. Seriously. What were they thinking? Deception will blind you and rob you of your inheritance when you think you have it.

Super comforting, right? The thought that we could have it all wrong regarding how we apply the Scriptures is slightly terrifying. It should be. There is a real danger in what you can't see. This is why we have headlights on our cars, flashing lights on towers, and yellow stripes on curbs.

Ignorance, in some cases, isn't bliss. It can hurt and even bring ruin. But the good news is that you can discern the difference between good and evil, even if the lines seem blurred. It is essential to know the truth and to do it, not being a hearer only like James talks about. We'll discuss that soon. But for now, I think it helps to know what we're up against.

Let's explore a little deeper into the mindset of the religious spirit. Jesus liked to refer to mindsets as leaven or yeast. He used a word picture to explain how these mindsets work their way into our thinking and, in turn, our behavior, like yeast in a batch of dough.

You might be familiar with the miracles of Jesus' feeding crowds of people with very little food. This miracle happened more than once during Jesus' ministry. In Mark's gospel, the people numbered 4,000. The disciples saw it and even served the multiplied food that day. The more they handed out to the hungry crowd, the more food appeared.

Can you imagine? They witnessed things no one had ever seen before. Then, when Jesus had finished speaking to the crowd, he crossed to the other side of the lake with his disciples. I bet they were so excited about the miracle they had just been a part of and were talking over each other about it, telling their side of the story, when suddenly someone realized that they never got bread to take with them on the boat. Bummer.

In the middle of this conversation about who was to blame for leaving lunch behind, Jesus interrupted them with a warning: "Be careful. Watch out for the yeast of the Pharisees" (Mark 8:13-21). Jesus wasn't as concerned about lunch as He was about teaching His students a valuable lesson. He was warning them about the teaching of the Pharisees, the teachings that consistently missed the mark and distracted from what actually mattered. This "leaven" or "yeast" Jesus spoke of symbolizes the influences on the mind that can rob us of our God-given identity and assignment. Our mindsets determine how we think and act. Jesus references another kind of leaven in Matthew's gospel: "Another parable He spoke to them: 'The kingdom of heaven is like leaven, which a woman took and hid in three measures of meal till it was all leavened.'" (Matthew 13:33)

Leaven, or yeast, in the natural world, spreads throughout the whole lump of dough and causes it to rise when heated. Who doesn't love a big fluffy loaf of fresh bread right out of the oven? My mouth is watering just thinking about it!

If the Kingdom is your dominant mindset, you begin to see your life through the lens of Heaven. It changes the way you think. Impossibility seems logical. Opportunities are born out of difficulty. As you become more and more "Heaven-minded," everything you encounter is colored by this new way of seeing things. Conversely, if the leaven of the Pharisees is filling your life, it will cause the way you think and live to be deficient in light of your inheritance in Jesus.

THE LEAVEN OF THE PHARISEES

The Pharisees were a strict sect within early Judaism that carefully adhered to the Mosaic Law, the law given to Moses at Mt. Sinai. They were a vital part of Jewish culture during the time of Jesus. When you read through the New Testament, you find the text smattered with confrontation between Jesus and these hyper-religious people. In the boat with His disciples, Jesus referred to the "leaven of the Pharisees." This represents the religious spirit. This is the "dragon."

When I say "religious spirit," I know there's an overuse of the term in some Christian circles, turning any difficulty into spiritual warfare and blaming every problem on the devil. I'm not advocating a superstitious faith where we make much of the enemy, reacting to his schemes rather than responding to our calling to partner with God to see His Kingdom realized.

But the religious mindset of the Pharisees is demonically inspired. Mindsets are not formed without ideas, and ideas come from somewhere. Strongholds aren't built without an architect.

The roots of the religious mindset are spiritual. There's no question. Demonically-inspired mindsets must be resisted and replaced with Kingdom thinking. And that change must start with us, examining our own deeply-held beliefs before we pin a badge of infamy on anyone else.

In Matthew 7, Jesus made it clear to us where the examination should begin: within ourselves:

> Do not judge, or you too will be judged. For in the same way you judge others, you will be judged, and with the measure you use, it will be measured to you. Why do you look at the speck of sawdust in your brother's eye and pay no attention to the plank in your own eye? How can you say to your brother, 'Let me take the speck out of your eye,' when all the time there is a plank in your own eye? You hypocrite, first take the plank out of your own eye, and then you will see clearly to remove the speck from your brother's eye.
>
> MATTHEW 7:1-5 NIV

Let's not go searching out the religious spirit in others. It inevitably leads us to operate in the wrong spirit, just like Jesus warned his disciples when they wanted to call down fire on those Samaritans. I'm grieved by how this religious language undermines and demonizes those we disagree with, even within the body of Christ.

This divisive rhetoric has us partnering with the Accuser (Revelation 12:10) and has no place in the Church of Jesus. The term "religious spirit" is not a weapon to be used against anyone. It is simply how I'm choosing to describe the effects of the religious mindset — spiritual leaven — on God's people and its impact on those outside of the family of God.

The religious mindset seeks to shut people out of the Kingdom. It aims to shut them down concerning the purpose of God for their lives, all in the name of religious piety and "sound doctrine." This attitude doesn't sit well with Jesus. We find Him constantly confronting the religious leaders of His day who were operating under this religious spirit.

Woe to you, teachers of the law and Pharisees, you hypocrites! You shut the door of the Kingdom of Heaven in people's faces. You yourselves do not enter, nor will you let those enter who are trying to.

MATTHEW 23:13 NIV

So, how do we recognize the religious mindset in our own lives? How do we spot it to avoid it and resist its influence? To kill the dragon, we must first be able to find it.

CHAPTER TWO
Law Over Love

I love cake. A good butternut layer cake is my favorite, with seven-layer chocolate coming in at a close second. Honestly, I've never been one to turn down any kind of cake, and it doesn't need to be my birthday or anyone else's. Any occasion will do for a good piece of cake!

While different cakes call for various recipes, the essential ingredients are the same. Any cake recipe has some flour, maybe eggs, water or milk, flavoring, and, of course, sugar.

But imagine what cake would taste like if you left out an ingredient. If you forgot the eggs, it would undoubtedly change the cake's consistency. If you chose not to put the water in, you'd have a dry burnt mess to clean up after cooking! If you skipped the flavoring, it would impact the taste of the cake, but you'd still have the sweetness of the sugar, making it palatable.

But, what if you didn't put sugar in the cake? First of all, a cake without sugar is not even cake! After bringing it out of the oven, it might smell like cake or look like cake, but the moment you take a bite, you will immediately know something essential is missing. A cake with no sugar? What's the point?!

Just as you would quickly recognize the absence of sugar in a cake, there is one primary red flag for spotting the religious spirit in our lives and others. If you've been around religion at all, you've probably experienced it. While you may not have immediately recognized it as the religious spirit, you've likely felt something a little off but couldn't pinpoint exactly what it was.

Countless times, I have heard a message in a church service, read a Christian book, overheard a spiritual conversation, or participated in one with no signs of error on the surface...yet something was off. If you dissect the communication's content, you will find no glaring heresy, doctrinal error, or deception. Even so, you just have a feeling that something is missing. Something about the exchange doesn't sit well with you.

After walking away, you might feel uneasy, angry, or confused. You ask God to reveal any wrong attitudes in you. After being unable to find any evidence for your feelings, you chalk it up to bad vibes, or you carry shame for feeling the way you feel. "Something must be wrong with me," you think.

If you've ever experienced this, you might discern something more profound than surface level. I've had this happen so many times I've lost count. I often dragged along shame and a heaviness, not mine to carry. After wrestling with this for years, I realized that most of the time, the issue wasn't with something inherently wrong. The problem was that something was missing.

THE SOMETHING THAT'S MISSING

Love. It's the missing ingredient wherever the religious spirit operates. Even if we have "good doctrine," even if we are "right." It is possible to be right and wrong at the same time. It is possible to be right in the wrong way. In fact, "sound doctrine" without love is not "sound" at all. The very foundation of truth is gone. It's misguided at best and demonic at worst. Give it a microphone or a platform, and it becomes deadly! The leaven of the Pharisees is a heavy burden to bear. It will always leave you drained and exhausted in your pursuit to please God in your own strength. Religion elevates law over love.

This lack of love within the Church is often manifested in an over-emphasis on the anger and judgment of God. As a result, entire denominations and camps of Christianity pride themselves in presenting a God of wrath to the world.

Granted, we can't simply pick and choose from the Bible those verses that we like concerning the love of God and dismiss those having to do with His judgment. He is a God of wrath (Deuteronomy 9:8; Romans 1:18) but the deeper you look into this part of His nature and character, the more you see. You'll ask more critical questions, like "Why would God get angry?" or "What makes Him mad?" It doesn't take a long look into Scripture to find an answer. King Solomon spells out seven things that the Lord hates in this proverb:

> There are six things the Lord hates — no, seven things He detests: haughty eyes, a lying tongue, hands that kill the innocent, a heart that plots evil, feet that race to do wrong, a false witness who pours out lies, a person who sows discord in a family.
>
> PROVERBS 6:16-19 NLT

What we must notice about God's anger is that it's never vengeful or flippant. Instead, the root of His wrath is His love. I know that sounds like an oxymoron. But think of it this way – God's wrath is directed at anything that keeps His absolute best from people.

Let's consider Proverbs 6. First, Solomon mentions "haughty eyes" as a trigger for God's anger. The phrase "haughty eyes" is a way of describing a prideful attitude. It should be obvious why God hates pride. It's the attitude that destroys a person. Pride blinds people to their need for God, cutting them off from saving grace and relationship with God. Pride separates God's created family from His presence for eternity. Of course God would be angry about that! He hates pride because He loves people.

The rest of the list overwhelmingly demonstrates that God is vehemently opposed to anything that brings destruction to people's lives. His wrath is real, and we shouldn't take it lightly. But it flows from His righteous judgment against sin. One day God will finally and ultimately deal with sin and its effects.

That's great news. The unfortunate part is that anyone who refuses His kindness and rejects His free gift of salvation, choosing to identify themselves with sin rather than the Father, will ultimately be dealt with as well. For those who have received the gift of saving mercy and grace, their very identities become one with Jesus. By contrast, those who reject Him can only become sin itself and choose to be flushed out with everything concerning corruption and destruction.

God doesn't take delight in this at all. Instead, it grieves His heart immensely. Scripture is repetitive with bold proclamations of God's compassion and kindness toward those He loves, whether they love Him back or not. Here are just a few of those proclamations:

> But you, Lord, are a compassionate and gracious God, slow to anger, abounding in love and faithfulness.
>
> PSALM 86:15 NIV

> As a father has compassion on his children, so the Lord has compassion on those who fear Him.
>
> PSALM 103:13 NIV

> The Lord is gracious and righteous; our God is full of compassion.
>
> PSALM 116:5 NIV

The Lord is gracious and compassionate, slow to anger and rich in love. The Lord is good to all; he has compassion on all He has made.

PSALM 145:8-9 NIV

...God, who is rich in mercy, made us alive with Christ even when we were dead in transgressions...

EPHESIANS 2:4-5 NIV

He saved us, not because of righteous things we had done, but because of His mercy.

TITUS 3:5 NIV

Jesus said, "Father, forgive them, for they do not know what they are doing."

LUKE 23:34 NIV

Jesus' dying words bleed with tender compassion. He makes it clear that He loves those who hate Him and will give everything to restore humanity to Himself. The gospel writer John wrote about this love he had experienced firsthand:

In this the love of God was made manifest among us, that God sent His only Son into the world, so that we might live through Him. In this is love, not that we have loved God but that He loved us and sent His Son to be the propitiation for our sins.

1 JOHN 4:9-10 ESV

John went on to give the familiar title "God is love." This isn't the picture of God that religion paints. The religious spirit would rephrase it to read, "God is wrath." I've even had well-meaning people get defensive when I suggest the importance of communicating the love and mercy of God. I'm often met with, "Yeah, but...."

Now, I get where they're coming from. There has been a lot of "easy-believism" in the Church. But if your gut reaction to the topic of God's love is, "Yeah, but...." I'm not sure you've fully grasped the beauty of that love.

Take the Apostle Paul, in his former life as Saul, who was one of the most religious people on the planet. When he got knocked off his horse on the road to Damascus — on his way to kill Christians — he suddenly became aware of a God quite unlike the one he intended to serve. It took three years in the desert to get religion out of Paul. And in the end, he could pray for the Ephesians to experience the love he had experienced:

> I pray that out of His glorious riches He may strengthen you with power through His Spirit in your inner being, so that Christ may dwell in your hearts through faith. And I pray that you, being rooted and established in love, may have power, together with all the Lord's holy people, to grasp how wide and long and high and deep is the love of Christ, and to know this love that surpasses knowledge—that you may be filled to the measure of all the fullness of God.
>
> EPHESIANS 3:16-19 NIV

You might be familiar with most of the accounts of Jesus' ministry, especially if you've heard them all your life. There is a tendency for the miraculous to become commonplace in our minds. But let's revisit this amazing miracle in John 5:1-9.

Lying on a mat by the pool of Bethesda was a man who had been paralyzed for thirty-eight years. We don't know his name. We don't even know what happened to him. Maybe he was in an accident that left him unable to walk. We can imagine how hard life was for this man.

His only hope for healing was to lay by a pool near the Sheep Gate in Jerusalem and hope for a miracle. You see, legend told of an angel that would come and stir the waters there and that anyone who entered the water during this supernatural event would be healed. This was a well-known legend because the area was filled with people with various ailments and disabilities. Desperation was palpable. Any perceptible change in the water's surface would send them all scrambling to the water to find relief. But this man was confined to his mat, unable to get there fast enough. Someone always beat him to it. Imagine the disappointment he must have felt daily with no one to help him do the only thing he could think of to get well.

Here is where he meets Jesus. The Rabbi does something perhaps no rabbi has done before. First, he listens to the man's story. Then he asks a question that sounds like the most insensitive and offensive question one could ask. "Do you want to get well?"

The man tells the story he had probably told countless times about why he could never reach the water. He has no one to help him. He is helpless. Then Jesus, full of compassion for the man, tells him, "Get up! Pick up your mat and walk." And he does.

He has been waiting for a miracle for no telling how long. And on this day, his Miracle walks right up, sees him, asks him if he wants to get well, and heals him on the spot. It all causes quite a stir at the pool. No pun intended.

I'm sure it inspired awe and love for Jesus in some who were gathered. But, on the other hand, it probably confused many, and it was perhaps even a little scary for others. You would think that of all the people who witnessed this miraculous event, the ones who would be the most overjoyed by it would be the people who claimed to represent God to the people, the religious leaders. (You probably know where this is going already.) And their response? "It is the Sabbath; the law forbids you to carry your mat" (John 5:9-10).

Really? A man who has suffered for thirty-eight years, broken, abandoned, forgotten, and cast aside, has been instantly and miraculously restored to complete health, walking for the first time in over three decades, carrying the mat under his arm that he laid on for years. Still, all the religious leaders can say is, "Excuse me, sir. You can't carry your mat on the Sabbath."

Wow. It sounds ridiculous, right? And it is, but not to those convinced that their job was to be the "enforcers." They had grounds for their accusation. After all, one of the reasons that their ancestors were led into captivity was their refusal to honor the Sabbath (Nehemiah 13:17-18; Ezekiel 20:24). Remembering the Sabbath and keeping it holy was one of the "Big 10," right (Exodus 20:8)? The law they were enforcing was actually law from God. It was a clear command in the Torah:

> There are six days when you may work, but the seventh day is a day of sabbath rest, a day of sacred assembly. You are not to do any work; wherever you live, it is a sabbath to the LORD.
>
> LEVITICUS 23:3 NIV

You see, the problem was not with the law itself. The problem, in this case, was a misapplication of the law. It was true that the law prohibited working on the Sabbath, but these zealous religious leaders had redefined what "working" actually meant. To be fair, they were just following the guidelines of their religious instruction. The Jewish fathers before them had tried to make the law more practical to daily life, spelling out for everyone what it looked like applied to everyday habits.

They might have been well-meaning in their approach. The problem is that God never asked them to do this. His law didn't need "improvement." And now, years later, the enforcers of this strict application of the law were nitpicking everything down to the tiniest detail, to the point of refusing to celebrate a miracle because it seemed to conflict with a commandment (well, their version of it, anyway). They were blinded by their zealous adherence to what they thought was right. This is what religion without love does. It blinds. Law without love is not only misguided—it's downright dangerous. Beneath the shimmering surface of piety, the heart of the dragon beats, embodying the true nature of the religious spirit, where a love for orthodoxy surpasses love for people.

This isn't the only time Jesus heals on the Sabbath. We find Him repeatedly doing miracles on the day of rest. He heals Peter's mother-in-law on the Sabbath (Mark 1:29-31), restores a withered hand in the actual synagogue on the Sabbath (Mark 3:1-6), heals a blind man, a disabled woman, a man with swollen limbs, all on the Sabbath (John

9:1-16; Luke 13:10-17, 14:1-6). On another occasion, He casts a demon out of a guy who was shouting in the synagogue, again, on the Sabbath (Mark 1:21-27). Likely, these accounts in Scripture aren't an exhaustive list of Sabbath-day healings and miracles. Applying the words of the prophet Isaiah to Himself, Jesus once stood in the synagogue and said:

> The Spirit of the Lord is on me, because He has anointed me to proclaim good news to the poor. He has sent me to proclaim freedom for the prisoners and recovery of sight for the blind, to set the oppressed free, to proclaim the year of the Lord's favor.
>
> LUKE 4:18 NIV

The "work" of bringing the good news to the poor, freeing prisoners, opening blind eyes, and setting the oppressed free is not the kind of work the law was prohibiting. So maybe God is actually good, and the purpose of the law was deeper than just keeping His people under control. Paul explains in his letter to the Galatians. He writes:

> But when the right time came, God sent his Son, born of a woman, subject to the law. God sent him to buy freedom for us who were slaves to the law, so that He could adopt us as His very own children. And because we are his children, God has sent the Spirit of His Son into our hearts, prompting us to call out, "Abba, Father." Now you are no longer a slave but God's own child. And since you are His child, God has made you His heir.
>
> GALATIANS 4:4-7 NLT

The Father's purpose from the beginning was to get His kids back. The origin of the law was a heart of love, the love of a good Father. One of the most important conclusions we can come to is that every command of God is rooted in His unfathomable love for us.

This love, my friends, is the antithesis of the religious spirit. If you are reading this and have fallen for the lie that your good works keep you in good graces with God, you possibly have come to a place of disillusionment that you'll never be enough for Him. If you doubt that He could and would love you in your brokenness, let these beautiful words from Brennan Manning sink into the depths of your soul:

> Your Christian life and mine don't make any sense unless, in the depth of our beings, we believe that Jesus not only knows what hurts us but, knowing, seeks us out whatever our poverty, whatever our pain. His plea to His people is, 'Come now, wounded, frightened, angry, lonely, empty, and I'll meet you where you live. And I'll love you as you are, not as you should be, because you're never going to be as you should be.' Do you really believe this? With all the wrong turns you made in your past... the mistakes, the moments of selfishness, dishonesty and degraded love? Do you really believe that Jesus Christ loves you? Not the Person next to you, not the church, not the world. But that He loves you—beyond worthiness and unworthiness, beyond fidelity and infidelity. That he loves you in the morning sun and in the evening rain. Without caution, regret, boundary, limit. No matter what's gone down, He can't stop loving you. This is the Jesus of the Gospels.

CHAPTER THREE

Belief Over Experience

"God doesn't speak to us like that anymore because we have the Bible now." These words were etched into my thinking as a young boy by a well-meaning Sunday school teacher. That day's lesson was about Moses and his encounter with God in the burning bush. While I understand her intentions and don't blame her one bit for it, the thought of it never left me and informed how I saw God for most of my Christian life that followed.

As a kid with a wild imagination, the story of God speaking from a bush on fire to call Moses into His divine purpose was mysterious, magical, and awe-inspiring. But, the wonder that filled my young heart of a powerful yet personal God was interrupted by a new thought I'd never had before that moment: "God doesn't speak to us like that anymore."

I could almost imagine God retreating from the scene, slipping away into the mist, disappearing into His heavenly abode, now invisible and obscure. Suddenly, out of the dense fog, a Bible plops open before me, accompanied by a distant booming voice saying, "Good luck, kid!" (Okay, maybe that's a little dramatic, but I told you I had a vivid imagination.)

It was an innocent, albeit misguided, statement that sought to elevate the essential nature of the Scriptures. But I left the classroom that day with a tainted view of God, a lens that saw Him as unapproachable, impersonal, and even unpleasant. The dragon's dark magic had begun its work in my impressionable mind. For years, even as a believer, every truth I heard concerning the goodness of God and His love would come under immediate internal scrutiny. Deep down, I wondered if it was true. I certainly hoped it was, but I wasn't convinced.

Then one day, someone handed me a book that further solidified my wrong thinking. This book, which I quickly devoured, reinforced the belief that God was no longer active in our daily lives, especially when it came to anything miraculous. It wasn't that God couldn't do miracles today; instead, He had chosen not to. The book was full of accusations and ridicule against people who claimed to hear the voice of God or be led by "impressions" from Him. According to the author, the idea that God was still speaking and moving miraculously today was lousy theology at best and demonically inspired at worst.

The foundation of this kind of thinking is a doctrine known as cessationism, the view that all miraculous gifts of the Holy Spirit, such as prophecy, healing, and tongues, were only in operation before the establishment of the early Church, specifically before the formation of the Bible we have today. Cessationists don't deny that God still does miracles. Many people who hold this view believe God can do whatever He wants regarding the miraculous.

Take the subject of healing, for example. Most cessationists believe God still heals; they wouldn't affirm the existence of the gift of healing. Most would probably hold to the conviction that God heals when He wills; therefore, believers don't have much to do with when or where it happens. Prayer for healing is often cushioned comfortably with a disclaimer like, "If it is Your will, Lord." In my opinion, it takes zero faith to pray this way because the ball is in God's court entirely, and there is no room for belief or action on the part of the person praying. The logical outworking of this thinking potentially leads one to abandon all responsibility to pray for the sick. Why would Christians pray about anything if the outcome was already settled? To be fair, there is a spectrum of practice within cessationism, and not all would agree on what it looks like practically in church life.

But is there any biblical evidence for the cessationist view? The most common argument is in 1 Corinthians 13, where Paul tells the church at

Corinth that when "the perfect comes," there will be no use for prophecy or any other "miraculous" gifts. To the cessationist, "the perfect" means the completed version of the Bible (canonization) or the maturity of the Church. But both the argument for the completed canon and the maturity of the Church are weak suppositions because they are merely inferences from the text rather than explicitly stated in the text. Perhaps a more accurate understanding, and one rooted in reasonable biblical interpretation, is that "the perfect" Paul speaks of is the second coming of Christ when we will see Him "face to face" (1 Corinthians 13:12).

Another common argument for the cessation of certain gifts is the presupposition that the gifts primarily served to authenticate the authority of the original apostles. So, the reasoning is when the apostles died, so did the gifts. While signs and wonders indeed accompanied the ministry of the apostles, it was not the primary proof of apostleship. Nowhere in the New Testament are supernatural phenomena said to be a sign attesting to the apostles' authority but rather a proof of the authority of the gospel message itself. Not to mention, there are plenty of accounts in Scripture of believers who were not apostles who operated in these supernatural abilities. In Acts 6:8, we read of Stephen, a deacon, not an apostle, doing "great wonders and signs among the people." And upon his death, he saw a vision of Jesus Himself "standing at the right hand of God" (Acts 7:55).

He is not named an apostle, even though he had these powerful experiences. Another deacon in the early church named Philip healed the sick and cast out demons, and yet only the title "deacon" is conferred on him (Acts 6:5; 8:7). When it comes to the gift of prophecy, we read that the same Philip had four daughters who prophesied as well (Acts 21:9). We can confirm that many non-apostles were regularly prophesying in meetings because Paul lists the gift in Romans 12:6 and brings correction in his letter to the Corinthians, not forbidding it, but rather establishing guidelines (1 Corinthians 14). The same goes for the gift of tongues and the interpretation of tongues in the same letter to the same church.

A continuationist, by contrast, believes that the miraculous is happening today and that all the gifts of the Holy Spirit are still operative. Of course, anyone who thinks this is true would certainly pray with more faith than someone who doesn't. A continuationist would even consider praying for the sick, for example, personal responsibility in light of the continuation of these gifts.

I'm not trying to win converts over to the continuationist side by pointing out differences between these two schools of thought. I'm highlighting the fact that experience matters. Our beliefs must look like something. They must affect the way we live.

Cessationism was the perspective of the author of the book I was given as a college student. Granted, many of the people and practices the author condemned represented the fringe of the Christian community, and of course, there will always be doctrinal errors wherever you look in the Body of Christ. But this argument presented, like with so many divisive issues, is a "straw man," only choosing the blatant errors to characterize the whole. It's a classic example of "throwing the baby out with the bathwater." But at the time, I just believed what I read out of respect for the author, a world-renowned Bible teacher.

The most potent argument in his polemic against the miraculous was simple: "Experience is not a valid test of truth." Let's look closer at that statement. First of all, it is absolutely true. We can, in no way, elevate experience over the truth of Scripture. If we have an experience that violates or challenges the authoritative word of God, however spiritual or powerful it may be, it is to be rejected. Likewise, if we think we have received a word from God that directly opposes the inspired Scriptures, we have certainly not received it from God. He never has, and never will, violate His own Word.

Unfortunately, many in the Church have claimed to have a prophetic word from God that has been proven unbiblical. Many have also claimed to have some special gift, such as healing, and have fallen into a questionable or even sinful lifestyle, not only disgracing themselves and the Church as a whole but also bringing doubt to the validity of the gift in which they claimed to operate.

People see this happen in the Church and quickly point a finger. "Aha! See there!" they'll say. "He's a false prophet! There's another example of why this stuff isn't real."

But many people believe that the gifts of the Holy Spirit are still in operation today and don't spin off into heresy. Everyone with room in their theology for the supernatural isn't a nut job! Instead, brilliant men and women have concluded that God still empowers His Church with all the beautiful gifts of the Spirit. I believe theological acrobatics are required to conclude that God no longer speaks or acts in miraculous ways in our world. The activity of the Holy Spirit is evident in Church history.

Justin Martyr (c. AD 100-165) spoke of the gift of prophecy as a present reality in the Church's life long after the original apostles had passed. Furthermore, Irenaeus (c. AD 120-202), the most influential second-century theologian, wrote of miracles, exorcisms, visions, prophecy, and even resurrection. Other notable figures in the second and third centuries, such as Tertullian, Clement of Alexandria, Hippolytus, and Eusebius, all confirm the presence of such spiritual activity during their lifetimes and, in most cases, endorse it. It doesn't end there. It extends through the fourth century among the Cappadocian Fathers. It is present throughout the Middle Ages through saints like Gregory the Great (540-604), Bernard of Clairvaux (1090-1153), Francis of Assisi (1182-1226), and Catherine of Siena (1347-1380).

The Protestant Reformation saw its share of the miraculous power of the Spirit. John Knox (c. 1514-1572) spoke of the gift of prophecy and even operated in it occasionally. Robert Bruce (1554-1631) not only exercised incredible spiritual discernment and prophesied many things that would come to pass; but he was also known for his extraordinary grace for seeing those with epilepsy and mental illness healed when he would pray for them.

I could go on and on with examples stretching into the era of colonial America to the present day, but I'll leave it for now since there's a wealth of information on the subject. The real purpose of this power is not to prove apostleship or doctrine or to make anyone rich by becoming a famous healing evangelist. The point of the gifts of the Spirit and miracles is to attest to the power of the gospel of Jesus Christ.

If that gospel was accompanied by supernatural power in its earliest expression, the gospel is the same today, and thus, the same power is needed today more than ever. Yet large swaths of the modern Christian community reject miraculous activity. This is one of the most unfortunate mindsets that has crept into the Church. What if this kind of power is for us today? And what if God intends for His Church to impact our world with the message of the gospel and demonstrate it in power? Paul says in his letter to the Corinthians:

> And so it was with me, brothers and sisters. When I came to you, I did not come with eloquence or human wisdom as I proclaimed to you the testimony about God. For I resolved to know nothing while I was with you except Jesus Christ and Him crucified. I came to you in weakness with great fear and trembling. My message and my preaching were not with wise and persuasive words, but with a demonstration of the Spirit's power, so that your faith might not rest on human wisdom, but on God's power.
>
> 1 CORINTHIANS 2:1-5 NIV

Wouldn't it be a shame to avoid something promised to you? Wouldn't it be sad to miss out on your full potential in Christ to make Him known on Earth? What if you could spend your entire life knowing about the power of God but never experiencing it? That is one of the worst scenarios I can imagine.

I'm not trying to single out my cessationist brothers and sisters. I'm just using this viewpoint to illustrate the possibility of knowing the truth without accompanying experience. While it may be true that experience is not a valid test of truth, at some point, there ought to be an experience that corroborates our beliefs. What good is knowledge that has no practical outworking in our lives? We cannot dismiss the truth of Scripture based on our bad experiences, either.

Here's my point: it's possible to know something with every fiber of your being and yet have zero experience with it. The dragon entices individuals with the allure of a well-defined belief system, offering a sense of security and a neatly packaged framework that erases all mystery.

Religion has an answer for everything but lacks experiential knowledge. Paul describes this mindset in his second letter to Timothy:

> But understand this, that in the last days there will come times of difficulty. For people will be lovers of self, lovers of money, proud, arrogant, abusive, disobedient to their parents, ungrateful, unholy, heartless, unappeasable, slanderous, without self-control, brutal, not loving good, treacherous, reckless, swollen with conceit, lovers of pleasure rather than lovers of God, having the appearance of godliness, but denying its power. Avoid such people. For among them are those who creep into households and capture weak women, burdened with sins and led astray by various passions, always learning and never able to arrive at a knowledge of the truth.
>
> 2 TIMOTHY 3:1-7 ESV

Paul urges Timothy to avoid the kind of thinking that prides itself on knowing about God but not having an experiential, real relationship with Him. Learning and education are fundamentally needed in the Church. I'm a huge proponent of not "checking our minds at the door" regarding the Christian life. Jesus was not, and certainly is not, opposed to growing in knowledge. He was educated in the Torah in his local synagogue, like every other Galilean Jew. It was there that He learned how to read it, memorize it, and apply it. Such was Jewish life at the time. Jesus had a robust theological education, as did Paul and many others.

Education is essential and should be pursued to understand how to interpret and apply the Bible to our lives. Even so, what good is learning if we never actually arrive at our destination? And the destination is knowing Jesus, not just in theory, but personally – experientially.

After all, He is not a subject to be studied. He's a person to be known. He's the most fascinating person you'll ever meet. Jesus Himself warned the religious leaders of pursuing knowledge without an experiential relationship, and I appreciate Eugene Peterson's paraphrase of the passage:

> You have your heads in your Bibles constantly because you think you'll find eternal life there. But you miss the forest for the trees. These Scriptures are all about me! And here I am, standing right before you, and you aren't willing to receive from me the life you say you want.
>
> JOHN 5:39-40 MSG

Jesus was cautioning those competent, well-educated experts who examined the Scriptures not to miss the point. May His gentle yet firm rebuke also fall upon the soft soil of your heart. Friend, the goal is not knowing more about Jesus. The goal is Jesus Himself. And, just as He called the tax collector Matthew to leave his booth and the sons of Zebedee away from their fishing nets, today He is calling you to wriggle out of your religious backpack — to lay down all of the books, degrees, and titles to follow Him with everything you have, and in doing so, truly know Him.

CHAPTER FOUR

Tradition Over Truth

Just like we can elevate belief over experience, if we aren't careful, we can also place tradition over the timeless truths of Scripture. The religious leaders of Jesus' day were notorious for this! One over-the-top example of this is found in Mark's gospel.

One day some Pharisees traveled from Jerusalem to check up on all this Jesus business they'd heard about. The second they arrived, they noticed something they didn't approve of at all. The disciples weren't washing their hands before eating. So, of course, they felt they had to immediately take this up with the Rabbi responsible for these disciples. They confronted Jesus about it:

> So the Pharisees and teachers of the law asked Jesus, "Why don't your disciples live according to the tradition of the elders instead of eating their food with defiled hands?"
>
> MARK 7:5 NIV

You read that right. The religious leaders were policing others' hand-washing habits! Granted, this was a very serious thing to the religious leaders and, obviously, something they felt deeply enough to bring up in a public rebuke aimed at Jesus and His disciples. But this was about more than a personal hygiene choice. Ceremonial hand-washing, in the minds of these leaders, was a righteous act, a serious matter that communicated faithfulness to God. They couldn't understand how any good Jew would not follow such an important command.

But was it God's command? Notice the text explains that this was a tradition of the elders. In reality, the very thing the Pharisees and teachers of the law thought was so important was not a command of God at all but rather an addition to His commands. It had been passed down through the generations and slowly became more than a suggestion. It was now a hard and fast rule that could not be broken.

At first thought, I wanted to give these religious leaders a break. After all, they were doing what they'd been told. But then I think about the context of the rebuke in this passage. The gospel writer is setting a scene for us here.

Picture it. A crowd was almost always gathered around Jesus in public, and in that crowd were the broken, the sick – ones who actually wanted to be with Him or needed something from Him. Then there were the curious, who just came out to see what all the fuss was about. And finally, there were the religious. (Sigh.) The religious people that showed up often seemed to do so for one purpose, to trap and humiliate Jesus. If they could catch Him making a mistake or cause Him to give a wrong answer, they could justify their jealousy and hatred toward him, and they would be right in the eyes of the people.

The goal was always simple: shut Jesus up, and shut Him down. That's exactly what is happening in this instance. They showed up that day with eyes peeled, looking for anything they could use in their accusations against Him.

"Aha! We've got Him now!" Or so they thought. The response from Jesus was probably enough to give them whiplash:

> He replied, "Isaiah was right when he prophesied about you hypocrites; as it is written:
>
> 'These people honor me with their lips, but their hearts are far from me. They worship me in vain; their teachings are merely human rules.' You have let go of the commands of God and are holding on to human traditions." And He continued, "You

have a fine way of setting aside the commands of God in order to observe your own traditions!"

MARK 7:6-9 NIV

Jesus explained that the rules they were so set on enforcing were causing people to miss the point entirely. These rules weren't helping people connect with God at all. Instead, they were driving them away from God and distracting people from the commands He had given them. The point of the law was to reveal the heart in the first place, not to clean it up. In the following verses, He says:

'...Listen to me, everyone, and understand this. Nothing outside a person can defile them by going into them. Rather, it is what comes out of a person that defiles them.' After He had left the crowd and entered the house, His disciples asked him about this parable. 'Are you so dull?' He asked. 'Don't you see that nothing that enters a person from the outside can defile them? For it doesn't go into their heart but into their stomach, and then out of the body.' (In saying this, Jesus declared all foods clean.) He went on: 'What comes out of a person is what defiles them. For it is from within, out of a person's heart, that evil thoughts come—sexual immorality, theft, murder, adultery, greed, malice, deceit, lewdness, envy, slander, arrogance and folly. All these evils come from inside and defile a person.'

MARK 7:14-23 NIV

Oh, the irony. Their insistence upon washing hands, cups, and pitchers to make one "clean" was missing the point entirely. A dirty heart can't be cleaned up with hand-washing. Purity results from faith and trust in God, but religion has always flipped the script and made it about behavior modification. Something like ceremonial hand-washing may seem silly, but if we look deeper into the traditions we hold dear, ours can be just as ridiculous. Take worship preferences, for instance.

The Church has often divided over the how of worship and neglected the why.

WINDS OF CHANGE

In my twenties, I started my first full-time position as a worship leader in a small rural church in Alabama. I loved that church and still do. My family and I experienced the love and care of a church family over those eight years. Looking back at my time there, I'm amazed at how much God did in that little church. I'm grateful for that season and those people.

At first, we only had a piano and an organ, and I stood on the stage calling out hymn numbers and waving my arm in the air as I led the songs in my dress shirt — and, most importantly — a necktie. That's what worship looked like in that church. It had been that way for years. It was the only worship experience I had ever experienced as well, so we kept trucking along, doing it the same way for about a year. Then, one morning, the pianist approached me and said, "Hey. I've been praying about it, and due to some changes in my life, I think it's time for me to step down from playing the piano here."

After thanking her for her years of service, my next step was to find a new pianist. As I wondered who could fill this role, I thought, "I play piano! I love singing while playing. I can lead from the piano." So I spun that beautiful baby grand piano around one Sunday so that it faced the people in the pews and led the songs while playing the piano. It worked, and it was fun. After the service, a man approached me and asked,

"When are we going to get a piano player?"

"Well, I guess we have one!" I replied, thinking I was making a good joke. His face didn't reciprocate my humor. Instead, he just blankly stared back at me.

"We've always had a piano player. And a song leader is supposed to stand up there!" he said, pointing to the stage.

It seemed odd that anyone could be so stuck in their ways that something like this would upset them. But the truth is, I had plenty of my own religious ideas that I believed just because I had always believed them. And none of them were rooted in the Bible. They were more traditions than anything else. That's what happens with traditions we hold dear. They become our comfort. Traditions can be "what we've always done," and messing with that can be uncomfortable. Or even feel wrong.

Over the next several years, we slowly implemented changes in that church's worship. By year eight, it was no longer just me up front. Instead, a team of musicians and singers helped lead us in weekly worship, and I wasn't the only one leading the songs. As a result, the music became more lively, and the people became more expressive in their worship, clapping and raising their hands.

During those years, I tried my best to move our church forward, welcoming a new generation of worshipers while still honoring the past and its people. It's a difficult job, and I applaud anyone who has done it well. I'll admit, in my zeal to move the church into a new era, I didn't do everything right, especially explaining the "why" behind the changes I was making.

One day while I was working around the church, a woman asked to speak with me. She was visibly distraught. I knew this conversation wouldn't be fun, so I centered myself emotionally as best I could, prayed a little prayer under my breath, and invited her to sit with me. I listened intently as she vacillated back and forth between anger and sadness in response to what was happening to her church. The more she talked, the more emotional she became. I knew her anger toward me came from a place of deep pain and fear. After several minutes, she paused, and with a red face and tears welling up in her eyes, she asked, "Why can't we just do it like we used to?"

Everything she held dear was changing right before her eyes. She had grown up with church looking and sounding a certain way, and she had come to know God in that environment. To her, changing the way we worshiped was, at best, cheapening something beautiful and holy and, at worst, destroying it.

I've done the same thing in my history with God. Traditions are part of the human experience. We love our traditions, and many of them are helpful and beautiful. But in honoring them, we cannot hold onto the past and miss that God is moving us forward. When a tradition competes for my love for God, it has to go. When it becomes God to me, it has to go.

SACRED COWS

I use this example of music because these conversations have become commonplace in the Church. The typical response is to jump on the "traditional" train or, on the other end of the spectrum, the "modern." Those who love the traditional expression of church worship like to accuse the other side of making it about performance, what with those fog machines and all! The more contemporary crowd loves to bemoan the monotonous nature of traditional churches, which they say are "stuck in their ways" and unwilling to embrace change.

Here's the thing: both sides are probably correct on certain points, but both sides are wrong on others. This may come as a shocker, but the enemy couldn't care less about what side of the argument you're on. His ultimate desire is to keep us distracted over things that don't matter. As long as we keep digging our heels in over secondary issues, we'll never see true unity in the body of Christ. Unity demands diversity of thought. If we all think the same, we've become uniform, not unified.

As followers of Jesus and members of His Body, we must get honest with ourselves and ask some hard questions. What secondary issues are we allowing to divide us? What traditions are we elevating above truth? What methods have we turned into idols? What good things have we made into god things?

Certain places in Scripture carry particular importance in God's redemptive story. One such place is called Bethel. In the original language, the name Bethel means "house of God." It was a place of encounter, a holy place. That plot of land was where Abraham first called on the name of the Lord, building an altar there and sacrificing to the God of Israel (Genesis 13:3-4). His grandson, Jacob, found himself in the same place years later, on the run from his brother, Esau. There, he laid his weary head on a stone "pillow," slept, and dreamt of angels. God met with Jacob that night:

> When Jacob awoke from his sleep, he thought, "Surely the Lord is in this place, and I was not aware of it." He was afraid and said, "How awesome is this place! This is none other than the house of God; this is the gate of heaven." Early the next morning, Jacob took the stone he had placed under his head and set it up as a pillar and poured oil on top of it. He called that place Bethel.
>
> GENESIS 28:16-19 NIV

It was a life-changing moment, and Jacob didn't want to forget it. He memorialized this sacred space:

> Then Jacob made a vow, saying, "If God will be with me and will watch over me on this journey I am taking and will give me food to eat and clothes to wear so that I return safely to my father's household, then the Lord will be my God and this stone that I have set up as a pillar will be God's house, and of all that you give me I will give you a tenth.
>
> GENESIS 28:20-22 NIV

In the generations following, Bethel would become a place of national identity for the people of Israel, a place of holy visitation and gravity for them. Bethel became a pilgrimage site for God's people, where they would go in times of crisis to seek guidance from the Lord (Judges 20:18). Years later, as King Solomon's reign was ending, he began to take wives from other nations and religions, a direct violation of the law given to Moses for the people of Israel. In doing so, Solomon opened the door for idol worship in the nation. And within only one generation, things went south really quickly. After Solomon's death, the kingdom was split into two parts, Israel and Judah. Solomon's sons, Jeroboam and Rehoboam, would assume control of them, with Jeroboam ruling in the northern kingdom and Rehoboam in the south. Not only did this divide cause an irreparable schism in God's family, but both brothers, respectively, turned their nations away from God. And in 1 Kings, Jeroboam does the unthinkable:

> After seeking advice, the king made two golden calves. He said to the people, "It is too much for you to go up to Jerusalem. Here are your gods, Israel, who brought you up out of Egypt." One he set up in Bethel, and the other in Dan. And this thing became a sin; the people came to worship the one at Bethel and went as far as Dan to worship the other.
>
> 1 KINGS 12:28-30 NIV

Notice that Jeroboam didn't abandon Bethel or dismiss its importance. Instead, he used it as a foundation to build a new object of worship. He didn't change the story or the tradition. But worship shifted from the One true God to a god they could manage that still fit into their story. "Here are your gods, Israel, who brought you up out of Egypt" (1 Kings 12:28 NIV).

Devastating. A place of encounter had become a place of idolatry. Identifying with the physical location and the tradition of what had happened there had become more important to the people than God Himself.

The decision to erect this golden calf at Bethel began a chain reaction that led both kingdoms into more profound and prolific idolatry. As a result, the Assyrians invaded Israel's Northern kingdom, destroying and assimilating them into their empire. Judah (the Southern kingdom) would fare no better, as the Babylonians took them captive, destroying the temple in Jerusalem in 586 B.C.

I hope you are sensing the gravity of what the religious spirit is capable of when it gets into our thinking. It is anything but benign. Tradition isn't evil. Tradition can be an excellent avenue to help us contextualize Biblical truths and put them into practice. However, it becomes evil when we exalt it over truth and force others to do the same. When a dragon moves into a place, it drives out what was originally noble and virtuous, and the very air is poisoned with its breath.

Remembrance is important. God instructed His people to create memorials to revisit and recount the goodness of God in their history. One example is God's directive to construct a monument at the site of the Jordan River crossing into the Promised Land (Joshua 4:1-7). It is appropriate and wise to remind ourselves of our encounters with God. I often think back to the moments when God profoundly met me and changed my life.

I have an ongoing list of promises He's given me concerning my life and an app where I've archived prophetic words spoken to me through the years. This is a healthy habit. It keeps me going when I'm weary and maybe even disillusioned. Recounting my history with God – my testimony – infuses life into me. I can't understate the value it has added to my life.

I encourage you to create a system of organizing and revisiting these memories and promises in your own life. They'll keep your heart tender when adversity or disappointment threatens to harden you up. But the moment I attempt to recreate or memorialize what He's done in a way that elevates that experience over the present relationship — the reality of His presence and nearness in my life — I have entered dangerous territory. The drift toward idolatry is subtle. We must honor the history of His work in our lives without making that history the object of our worship.

This applies to our preferences surrounding styles of worship that have touched our hearts, places of worship that have helped us grow, people who have significantly impacted us, helpful methods, or anything else. I know it's a fine line to walk. But so is everything else in this life. We must fix our gaze on Jesus, connect with His heart, and lean into His words of life, which will always bring course correction when needed. Any advancement in human history has required us to let go of the past to embrace future possibilities. God is a God of history. He's a generational God, and He doesn't change.

He's also a God who is doing something new. "See, I am doing a new thing! Now it springs up; do you not perceive it? I am making a way in the wilderness and streams in the wasteland" (Isaiah 43:19 NIV). There is an art to embracing the future without dishonoring the past. There is a delicate balance between looking ahead and appreciating our origins. But the reality is, things change. The sooner we accept that, the better prepared we are to carry the next thing God is doing. To make a new wineskin, you must kill a cow, usually a sacred cow.

CHAPTER FIVE

Avoidance Over Influence

Have you ever heard the phrase, "Bad company corrupts good morals?" This idea actually comes from the Bible. When Paul exhorts the Church at Corinth, "Do not be deceived: 'Bad company ruins good morals'" (1 Corinthians 15:33 ESV), it's believed that Paul was using a popular phrase of his day.

I imagine this phrase being first spoken by someone's grandmother in antiquity, firmly admonishing a grandchild to be careful about who they were running the streets with. This is good advice for anyone, I suppose. Paul was referring to those in the faith community who were beginning to cast doubt on the resurrection of Jesus. "Don't hang around those people, or you'll start believing them," was the point he was trying to convey to the impressionable young Corinthian church.

It's true. If we aren't watchful, we can be influenced by voices and opinions that oppose the values of the Kingdom of God, and before we know it, we are down a path in our thinking that we never intended to walk. But, in light of this, how do we reconcile our responsibility to be cautious with our commitment to influence the world around us? How do we live in the tension of being in the world but not of it? Let's look at how the Master Himself did it.

I find it interesting that people with complicated issues always surrounded Jesus. He often found Himself directly in the path of the most hopeless and even rejected by society. But Jesus never took His cues from culture, especially the religious crowd. This is apparent in how He interacted with a leper:

> When Jesus came down from the mountainside, large crowds followed him. A man with leprosy came and knelt before Him and said, "Lord, if you are willing, you can make me clean." Jesus reached out His hand and touched the man. "I am willing," He said. "Be clean!" Immediately he was cleansed of his leprosy.
>
> MATTHEW 8:1-3 NIV

I love the boldness of this man to come to Jesus. At this point in history, there was a stigma associated with leprosy, as in some parts of the world today. While there have been some exaggerations in modern times concerning the stigma of leprosy at the time, the fact remains that it was something to be avoided. In the Law, the instructions were clear for how someone with a skin disease interacted with their community: "Those who suffer from a serious skin disease must tear their clothing and leave their hair uncombed. They must cover their mouth and call out, 'Unclean! Unclean!'" (Leviticus 13:45 NLT)

Interestingly, the "defiling disease" mentioned here doesn't refer to leprosy but broadens the term to include any skin disease. Unfortunately, the stigma of leprosy led many to believe it was evidence of God's judgment. As a result, many people who suffered from the condition have become a pariah, ostracized for no reason.

Modern-day humanitarians like Mother Theresa, who shocked the world by kissing the hands and foreheads of those with leprosy, have helped de-stigmatize the disease by loving and caring for people suffering from it, despite the immense fear surrounding it. Perhaps those like her have taken their cues from how Jesus treated this man in the passage.

So let's examine what happened here in light of the cultural moment where Jesus found Himself. Jesus touched a leper, and instead of Him becoming "unclean," the leper became clean.

What a beautiful moment. What a powerful statement. If Jesus can heal a leper, He can indeed heal a heart. Those who have experienced this extraordinary grace can identify with the words of the hymn writer Charles Wesley, "His blood can make the foulest clean; His blood availed for me!"

Whether touching the untouchable or loving the unlovable, Jesus was often criticized for his proximity to the brokenness around him. But His modus operandi was always relationship over reputation. He would rather have been seen as a "friend of sinners" than striving for status as a distinguished rabbi in the eyes of the religious leaders. As Matthew says, "The Son of Man came eating and drinking, and they say, 'Look at him! A glutton and a drunkard, a friend of tax collectors and sinners!' Yet wisdom is justified by her deeds."(Matthew 11:19 NIV)

There is a real danger in being "conformed to the world" (Romans 12:2). Don't get me wrong. But there is an equally severe error in avoiding "the world" to the degree that the Church robs the world of the life it was meant to bring to them. We owe the world the same encounter with God's grace we experienced. Jesus beautifully walked out a tension — a balance — for us to model, and by understanding our role as imagers of God, we become better equipped to do so.

The ironic thing about the leaven of the Pharisees is that avoiding culture is seen as a virtue, to separate oneself from the world to maintain holiness, rather than living out of a new identity in Christ and influencing the culture around us. The Kingdom life, to which we've been called, is a way of living that affects the culture from a place of holiness rooted in identity. In other words, it's about living from the reality that holiness is an "inside job" that works its way out, not the other way around. Perhaps our fear of being affected by the world (or appearing to be) has caused us to retreat from it instead of engaging it.

You cannot love that which you fear. The reality we fixate on will be the reality in which we live. It is a mindset issue. As we've learned, how we think informs how we interact with the world around us. The way I see it, two primary mindsets dictate how we live.

COMPETING MINDSETS

The first mindset is avoidance. This mindset is rooted in misplaced identity and purpose. When we believe lies about our identity in Christ, we start living in light of those lies. One of the biggest lies about our identity has to do with holiness.

The religious spirit touts holiness as external rather than internal. Therefore, according to religion, holiness must be maintained at all costs. And the only way to sustain outward holiness is to avoid anything and everything that might threaten that holiness. This starkly contrasts the holiness that is ours through the finished work of Jesus on the cross. The holiness we have because of salvation is not conditional. It's not based on our performance, goodness, or failures. It's more about who we are than what we do.

This is not to say we are not responsible for living holy lives. It just means that our new identity in Christ now informs how we behave. I like to see it this way. There is what I like to call "positional holiness," and then there is "practical holiness." Positional holiness has nothing to do with us. It has everything to do with what Jesus has done for us. Practical holiness is the functional walking out of what has been done within us. It involves living every day from our position as new creations in Him (2 Corinthians 5:17). Remaining connected to Him and living in obedience to Him helps us grow into Him and become holy in how we live.

Can you see fear creeping into the equation once again here? The avoidance mindset is rooted in fear. It's a fear of unholy influences and maybe even an unhealthy fear of God Himself. But another fear factor is at play here: the fear of man.

"What will people think of me?" is an all too common thought pattern that can consume us as humans, especially believers, when we listen to the dragon's whispers. "The fear of man lays a snare," according to the wisdom of Solomon (Proverbs 29:25 ESV). It's nothing but a trap.

If anyone were immune to the fear of man, you'd think the Apostle Peter would be. After all, he is known for his boldness, like the time he proclaimed that Jesus was the Messiah when no none else was willing to say it (Matthew 16:16). And don't forget when he suggested to the Son of God that dying for the world was a bad idea (Matthew 16:23), which resulted in a stern rebuke from Jesus. You know, the "Get behind me, Satan" mic drop? Or how about the time Peter's message to the crowds at Pentecost resulted in 3,000 people choosing to follow Jesus in one day? He was the poster child for boldness!

But then we find him in Antioch, confronted by Paul because he caved on a fundamental issue (namely, that circumcision was not required for those who professed faith in Jesus), all because he feared what people would think. Paul took issue with Peter's hypocrisy. Peter rolled into town and had dinner with some Gentile believers, but as soon as his Jewish friends showed up, he wouldn't be seen with them for fear of what the Jewish believers would think. He placed those non-Jewish believers on a lower level than his fellow Jewish believers, and it caused division in the Church (Galatians 2:14).

Paul wouldn't let this one slide, and he rebuked Peter openly. He later wrote, "This false teaching..." (the dependence upon the law and works) "is like a little yeast that spreads through the whole batch of dough!" (Galatians 5:9 NLT). Thank goodness they got that one worked out! It was a defining moment in the life of the early Church and led to the gathering known as the Jerusalem Council that set the record straight on the matter. In that council, saving grace was affirmed, and favoritism was crushed. But the whole ordeal goes to show how easy it is to fall into the trap of the fear of man.

The opposing mindset, and in my view, the Biblical one, is influence. It's rooted in the idea that we are called to influence the world around us with the values of the Kingdom of God. This way of thinking starts with an awareness of the assignment. But self-awareness must follow if we are to bring godly influence truly. We won't speak or act effectively if we don't think our influence matters.

We must also be firmly rooted in our true identity and hold fast to the conviction that holiness is an internal work resulting from God's work in us. And now, as new creations (2 Corinthians 5:17), we have a new assignment: to demonstrate the reality of the Kingdom to those who haven't found it yet. Paul's letter to the church at Philippi gives us some fantastic insight into what our identity and assignment look like as we influence this earth with the Kingdom:

> For our citizenship is in Heaven, from which we also eagerly wait for the Savior, the Lord Jesus Christ, who will transform our lowly body that it may be conformed to His glorious body, according to the working by which He is able even to subdue all things to Himself.
>
> PHILIPPIANS 3:20-21 NKJV

First of all, he identifies us as citizens of Heaven. So, we live on Earth but are citizens of another place. This echoed Jesus's remarks to Pilate when He said, "My Kingdom is not of this world..." (John 18:36). Imagine a family from Brazil who moves to the United States. They are still citizens of Brazil but are resident aliens in the nation where they now live. They may live and work in the United States, but their loyalties are to their government back home in their own country.

This is similar to how we live as citizens of Heaven. We live on Earth, work at our jobs, raise our families, and participate in nearly all aspects of life here on Earth, but our true allegiance lies with a King whose

Kingdom is other-worldly. The Greek word políteuma, translated as "citizenship," can also be translated as "colony."

This implies that we are like a commonwealth of citizens conducting our heavenly government's affairs, although we are here on earth. We are representatives of God's Kingdom here and now. And just as citizens of another country inevitably bring their own culture and customs with them and influence their temporary home, we influence those around us with the culture of Heaven. Or at least that's what we're supposed to be doing.

The National Peanut Festival is an annual event in my home state of Alabama that draws around 200,000 people annually from around the Southeast. You read that right. "The National Peanut Festival." That seems like a lot of people making a big deal of a peanut, huh? Well, considering that most of the peanuts grown in the United States are grown within a 100-mile radius of Dothan (where the festival is held), I guess you could say that the little peanut is a big deal around those parts! The festival celebrates the economic growth that peanut farming brought to the region and honors local peanut farmers. There are about ten days of concerts, amusement rides, animal attractions, livestock shows, a parade, and hundreds of vendors who set up booths selling food, handmade items, and much more. Plus tons and tons of peanuts, of course!

One year as I walked around the fairgrounds with my family, I passed a little booth full of items for sale. It caught my eye because the booth was so different from the rest of the little pop-up shops. I noticed that all the merchandise was from another culture, and the salespeople were, too. There were no shoppers inside the tent. It seemed to me at the time that no one was stopping by to shop because it just didn't appeal to anyone there. I'm sure there might have been a few patrons, but for the most part, the fairgoers were culturally about a million miles from what that shop owner was trying to sell them. I don't know who would buy anything I saw in that tent – probably not anyone who came to a Peanut Festival! I still remember the lady's face as she leaned over on one of the tables, looking disappointed.

In my mind, I immediately drew the connection between what I was witnessing and how many churches operate. As the church, we tend to "set up shop" in our communities and expect people to flock to them and "buy" what we're "selling." But then we get disappointed with the minimal results and sit down among ourselves and watch the crowds pass us by. We even resort to talking about the people on the outside. Surely they don't want what we've got because something's wrong with them. It couldn't be us or how we're presenting Jesus (or, I should say, representing Jesus).

I'm sure you catch my satire. But this story is such a parallel to our avoidance mentality. We often refuse to change our preferences to connect with those outside the faith. But we must find ways of bridging the cultural gap with the gospel of Jesus without compromising the truth of that gospel. It's possible, and many are doing it well. But the ones doing it well are often criticized by the larger church community and accused of "worldliness" or "selling out." Accusation is one of the favorite hobbies of a dragon.

The question is, how much do we want this generation? Are we willing to do whatever it takes to seek and save the lost? As the singer and songwriter Keith Green once said, "This generation of Christians is responsible for this generation of souls on earth." Sadly, the religious spirit has tricked us into avoiding the very people we've been sent to reach. He says exactly that in Luke: "And Jesus answered them, 'Those who are well do not need a physician, but those who are sick. I have not come to call the righteous but sinners to repentance.'" (Luke 5:31-32 ESV)

So, did Jesus avoid those who the religious people of His day considered outsiders? No. On the contrary, Jesus pursued them. He was found eating and drinking with them, spending time with them, and entering their world instead of demanding they enter His. Did this make Jesus a pushover? Did this prompt Jesus to ease up on His convictions and compromise? Not at all.

That's one of the many things I love about Jesus. He was full of grace and truth. When it came to sinners, He loved them enough to be misunderstood, even accused of being one of them! But He also wouldn't back down from the truth, calling men and women to repentance. Even though He didn't affirm their behavior He affirmed their humanity.

Loving people is simple. Overcoming the religious ruts in our thinking is trickier. First, we must be willing to change how we think to begin influencing others in love. After all, we don't want to be influencers for influence itself. We want to be kingdom influencers because people are His priority. So, Jesus, help us to love like You.

CHAPTER SIX

Doctrine Over Devotion

On a gorgeous spring day in a church in front of family and friends, I gave my vows to my bride, the love of my life. When I said my "I do's," I said yes to a covenant relationship with her that would weather any storm we would face. We didn't just express our love for each other that day. We made our intentions known that we would stick with it no matter what. Little did we know that the line "in sickness and in health" would be more than just words after one year of marriage.

In August of the following year, I received a cancer diagnosis that would prove my wife's commitment to me during months of chemotherapy and treatment. It was a challenging season, but I thank God that I'm cancer-free now. Even today, I am blown away by the devotion she showed me as she cared for, prayed for, and loved me during a tough time in our lives. Words don't get you very far regarding the harsh realities of disappointment, shattered dreams, and suffering.

Vows must be lived out. And vows must be more than platitudes. They must be born in a much deeper place — the heart. They must be expressed. Marriage vows are not what a person believes about their spouse but what they promise to be to their spouse. There is a difference.

Regarding our faith, we make introductory statements that define what we believe about God, the Scriptures, and the world around us. These doctrines are vital to staying on track and aligning our beliefs with God's unchanging truth. As believers and followers of Jesus, we are "confessional" at heart, regardless of religious affiliation.

The term "confessional" refers to the Church's commonly held beliefs through the centuries, rooted in the revelation of who God is and what He has done through the finished work of Jesus Christ and how that affects our lives in light of this glorious good news. Jesus affirmed Peter's confession that He was the Son of God:

> Now when Jesus came into the district of Caesarea Philippi, He asked his disciples, "Who do people say that the Son of Man is?" And they said, "Some say John the Baptist, others say Elijah, and others Jeremiah or one of the prophets." He said to them, "But who do you say that I am?" Simon Peter replied, "You are the Christ, the Son of the living God." And Jesus answered him, "Blessed are you, Simon Bar-Jonah! For flesh and blood has not revealed this to you, but My Father who is in Heaven. And I tell you, you are Peter, and on this rock I will build My church, and the gates of Hell shall not prevail against it.
>
> MATTHEW 16:13-18 ESV

After the ascension of Jesus into Heaven, the early Church adopted confessions to solidify and articulate what they believed. One of the earliest creeds is found in Paul's first letter to the church at Corinth:

> For I delivered to you as of first importance what I also received: that Christ died for our sins in accordance with the Scriptures, that He was buried, that He was raised on the third day in accordance with the Scriptures, and that He appeared to Cephas [Peter], then to the twelve. Then He appeared to more than

> five hundred brothers at one time, most of whom are still alive,
> though some have fallen asleep. Then He appeared to James,
> then to all the apostles. Last of all, as to one untimely born, He
> appeared also to me.

1 CORINTHIANS 15:3-8 ESV

The early existence of this creed in Paul's letter — within twenty-one years following the crucifixion — refutes the common criticism that the beliefs of the early church were corrupted and, therefore, unreliable. Instead, Paul was affirming that the gospel message had been handed down first-hand to him by those who saw the events with their own eyes.

Later, with the rise of Gnosticism and a host of other heresies creeping in, it became necessary for the early Church fathers to create a clear statement of belief for the global faith community. These two early creeds, developed around the same time, have become fundamental doctrines for the Church today.

The "Old Roman Creed," which was expounded upon and renamed the "Apostles' Creed," was used as early as the second century, and its earliest documented form is a letter written by Marcellus of Ancyra in Greek to Julius, the bishop of Rome, around AD 34.

THE APOSTLES' CREED

I believe in God, the Father almighty,
*   creator of Heaven and Earth.*
I believe in Jesus Christ, his only Son, our Lord,
*   who was conceived by the Holy Spirit*
*   and born of the virgin Mary.*
He suffered under Pontius Pilate,
*   was crucified, died, and was buried;*
*   he descended to Hell.*
The third day he rose again from the dead.

He ascended to Heaven
and is seated at the right hand of God the Father almighty.
From there he will come to judge the living and the dead.
I believe in the Holy Spirit,
the holy catholic* Church,
the communion of saints,
the forgiveness of sins,
the resurrection of the body,
and the life everlasting. Amen.

The original purpose of the Nicene Creed, drafted in 325 at the Council of Nicaea, was to address the Arian controversy, which revolved around the distinction between God the Father and the Son. To preserve the fundamental doctrine of the divinity of Jesus, the council crafted the Nicene Creed.

THE NICENE CREED

I believe in one God,
the Father almighty,
maker of Heaven and Earth,
of all things visible and invisible.
I believe in one Lord Jesus Christ,
the Only Begotten Son of God,
born of the Father before all ages.
God from God, Light from Light,
true God from true God,
begotten, not made, consubstantial with the Father;
through him all things were made.
For us men and for our salvation
he came down from Heaven,
and by the Holy Spirit was incarnate of the Virgin Mary,
and became man.

For our sake he was crucified under Pontius Pilate,
he suffered death and was buried,
and rose again on the third day
in accordance with the Scriptures.
He ascended into Heaven
and is seated at the right hand of the Father.
He will come again in glory
to judge the living and the dead
and his Kingdom will have no end.
I believe in the Holy Spirit, the Lord, the giver of life,
who proceeds from the Father and the Son,
who with the Father and the Son is adored and glorified,
who has spoken through the prophets.
I believe in one, holy, catholic* and apostolic Church.
I confess one Baptism for the forgiveness of sins
and I look forward to the resurrection of the dead
and the life of the world to come. Amen.

*that is, the true Christian church of all times and all places.

These words are so beautiful to me. They're grounding. They give me a healthy dose of humility when I consider that the gospel has been passed down for ages by men and women who believed it with all their hearts, some even to death. In his musical rendition of the Apostle's Creed, songsmith and saint Rich Mullins wrote of this beautiful gospel: "I did not make it. No, it is making me. It is the very truth of God and not the invention of any man."

Given the modern-day erosion of truth, even within the institution itself, I believe certain facets of the Church would do well to return to these creedal statements in church life. Words like these help us re-center and stay connected to something much bigger than ourselves in our small window of history. The great doctrines of the Christian faith anchor us when the winds and waves of moral relativism, deconstruction, and progressivism toss us to and fro.

Don't get me wrong. I'm all for deconstructing beliefs as long as they get constructed into something worth believing. And I'm all for being progressive. But if our progressive ideas cause us to drift from orthodoxy, I don't know if we can call that progress.

THE REAL THING

In all of our advancements, it might be tempting to think we have a corner on truth, that we suddenly have revelation on something the generations before us couldn't see or were not educated enough to understand. It might be tempting to re-invent the gospel to make it palatable to our modern culture. While it is wise to contextualize the message into our current culture, I find it nonsensical, perhaps even arrogant, to attempt to tear down a message that has suffered intense persecution, scrutiny, and ridicule through the ages yet still stands the test of time. We cannot improve upon the good news about Jesus. What we believe about it is crucial. Sound doctrine is essential.

Now, let's play the other side for a moment. Sound doctrine is good. But what good is sound doctrine if, in pursuit of it, we have forsaken the first and greatest commandment, to love God with everything? What if it is possible to believe all the right things but not have a heart that is truly changed by what we believe? What if it is possible to know about Jesus but not truly know Him? What if correct doctrine, as great as it is, is not good enough?

There is a real danger in being so orthodox that we find ourselves fighting for a God we don't know rather than loving a God who never asked us to fight for Him in the first place. When doctrine takes the place of devotion, there is a dragon afoot.

Imposing orthodoxy on others was the favorite hobby of the Pharisees. But as we can see here in Matthew's gospel, Jesus had a way of turning their orthodoxy on its head.

Then some Pharisees and teachers of the law came to Jesus from Jerusalem and asked, 'Why do your disciples break the tradition of the elders? They don't wash their hands before they eat!'

Jesus replied, "And why do you break the command of God for the sake of your tradition? For God said, 'Honor your father and mother' and 'Anyone who curses their father or mother is to be put to death.' But you say that if anyone declares that what might have been used to help their father or mother is 'devoted to God,' they are not to 'honor their father or mother' with it. Thus you nullify the word of God for the sake of your tradition. You hypocrites! Isaiah was right when he prophesied about you:

> These people honor Me with their lips, but their hearts are far from Me.
>
> They worship Me in vain; their teachings are merely human rules.
>
> MATTHEW 15:1-9 NIV

Of all the hard things Jesus said to the religious leaders of His day, the claim that their hearts were far from Him stings the most. He is essentially saying, "These guys are all talk. They don't really love me."

Ouch. The truth hurts. We can become so faithful to our theological frameworks and enamored with what we believe about this and that, and even in how we do church, we forget the main thing. The Pharisees loved their religious culture. Any observer could clearly see that. But they hated Jesus. Loving church is not the same thing as loving Jesus.

Love must look like something. Being in love is obvious. You can't hide it. Have you ever seen anyone in love? It's utterly ridiculous. Lovers walk around with goofy grins, hopelessly intoxicated with each other. My wife and I were that way when we started dating. By her admission, she walked around for a week so excited she was constantly ravenously hungry. As for me, I looked for every excuse to be with her. She's all I could think about.

Love does funny things to you. With the busyness of life, ministry, and raising three kids, the novelty of new love and butterflies in the stomach may have subsided, but I'm still crazy in love with my wife. We've been through difficult times, but I can honestly say that the longer we're married, the more crazy in love with her I become. It's a love that doesn't come and go. It withstands opposition and outlasts difficulty. And it shows. She knows it. I know it. Our kids know it.

Jesus said, "If you love me, you will keep my commandments" (John 14:15 ESV). I don't think He insinuates here that we prove our love by obedience, but instead that we obey because we love. Obedience is a byproduct of being in love with Jesus. There is no greater motivation for loving Him than knowing how much He loves us. And when we see that love for what it is, we cannot help but respond.

As helpful as personal discipline is when it comes to spending time with Him, obeying His Word, etc., the most extraordinary discipline is not the self-will to perform for Him but, rather, the discipline to remain in His love. The habit of slowing down and experiencing His love, bringing it to the forefront of our minds, letting it sink into our hearts like a healing medicine, bears the fruit of obedience. Jesus called this abiding: "I am the vine; you are the branches. Whoever abides in Me and I in him, he it is that bears much fruit, for apart from Me you can do nothing" (John 15:5 ESV).

What matters most is not what we know but whom. Who we know determines what we do and how we do it. Knowing Jesus and staying relationally connected to Him is the only way to live a life that matters in light of eternity. Eternity must be the backdrop for our life's purpose, or we will eventually run out of reasons to live. Without an ultimate "why," life is meaningless. He must be our why.

Judgment Day. It's not a topic you usually hear at the dinner table or even in church anymore. For whatever reason, it seems the Church doesn't talk about the coming day of judgment much, or if we do, we think of it as a day for the wicked to finally get what's coming to them. Am I right? But this topic shouldn't be avoided because it's a much better arrangement than we realize. For us who belong to Christ, Judgment Day is a day of reward. Yes, He is our Great Reward, but He also promises rewards to those who have been faithful:

> Yes, we are of good courage, and we would rather be away from the body and at home with the Lord. So whether we are home

or away, we make it our aim to please Him. For we must all appear before the judgment seat of Christ, so that each one may receive what is due for what He has done in the body, whether good or evil.

2 CORINTHIANS 5:8-10 ESV

Paul says that we will all stand before the judgment seat of Christ one day. What we've done will matter. Jesus further illustrates the point perfectly:

When the Son of Man comes in His glory, and all the angels with Him, he will sit on His glorious throne. All the nations will be gathered before Him, and He will separate the people one from another as a shepherd separates the sheep from the goats. He will put the sheep on His right and the goats on His left. Then the King will say to those on His right, "Come, you who are blessed by My Father; take your inheritance, the kingdom prepared for you since the creation of the world. For I was hungry and you gave Me something to eat, I was thirsty and you gave Me something to drink, I was a stranger and you invited Me in, I needed clothes and you clothed Me, I was sick and you looked after Me, I was in prison and you came to visit Me." Then the righteous will answer Him, "Lord, when did we see You hungry and feed You, or thirsty and give You something to drink? When did we see You a stranger and invite You in, or needing clothes and clothe You? When did we see You sick or in prison and go to visit You?" The King will reply, "Truly I tell you, whatever you did for one of the least of these brothers and sisters of Mine, you did for Me." Then He will say to those on His left, "Depart from Me, you who are cursed, into the eternal fire prepared for the devil and his angels. For I was hungry and you gave Me nothing to eat, I was thirsty and you gave Me nothing to drink, I was a stranger and you did not invite Me in, I needed clothes and you did not clothe Me, I was sick and in prison and you did not look after Me." They also will answer,

"Lord, when did we see You hungry or thirsty or a stranger or needing clothes or sick or in prison, and did not help You?" He will reply, "Truly I tell you, whatever you did not do for one of the least of these, you did not do for Me." Then they will go away to eternal punishment, but the righteous to eternal life.

MATTHEW 25:31-46 NIV

It is clear. As believers, we will be judged for our acts, not facts. As important as doctrine is, as it informs our behavior, we will not take a standardized test when we get to the judgment seat of Christ. We won't be tested for what we know.

We will be judged and rewarded for our deeds. That fact alone should stir us to good works. Jesus said in another place that those who have been forgiven of much love much, but those who are forgiven little love little (Luke 7:47). Do we see how immeasurable His love is for us? Let's serve Him from that awareness. He's not looking for impressive doctrinal purity as much as He is looking for undying devotion. Let's be people who love Him well.

CHAPTER SEVEN
Control Over Trust

everal years ago, during a season of preparation to plant a church, I
Sworked at a financial institution to make ends meet for our family
until we could move to our new city to begin the work God called us to
do. The CEO (I'll call him Tim) made an impression on me. You might
have the idea of a stereotypical bank president sitting behind a desk in a
suit and tie, tucked away from the public and his employees. (No offense
to any bankers reading this. Perhaps you've been sorely misrepresented
in movies!)

That's very different from what I experienced working for Tim. He
was upbeat, encouraging, and present. On any given day, he would pop
in and greet every department with a big smile on his face. He'd leave
with a chipper word like, "I appreciate all your hard work! You guys are
awesome!" I never heard anyone talk negatively about him during my
entire year there. He treated the employees with respect and care, and
we naturally returned the favor.

One day I had to visit another department to deliver some paperwork.
When I walked into the office, two ladies were having a conversation. I
first noticed that one of them, behind the desk, was reclined in her office
chair with her feet propped up on the desk. I delivered the paperwork
and stepped back into the doorway as we wrapped up our very brief
conversation. Because of where I was standing, I had a clear view of
the door at the end of the hallway, a view the reclining woman did
not have. I saw that door swing open and Tim approach in his brisk
jaunt. In hindsight, I probably should've let the ladies know who was

coming down the hall! But I didn't have time to think. Tim popped his head in the office doorway within seconds with a perky "Good morning, everybody!" The speed at which those feet came off that desk and that chair snapped upright would rival a major league fast pitch across home plate! Visibly shaken, the ladies went straight to work as they greeted him. I tightened my lips to keep from laughing at the sight of it. It provided me with some comic relief and taught me something.

As kind as Tim was, the presence of his authority was all it took to correct the situation. I see a parallel in our relationship with God. I believe that more can happen in His presence than in twenty years of "doing church." In my experience, one moment in His presence has changed me more times than I can count. Simply the awareness of His presence corrected my wrong thinking and attitudes. That's how He leads His people. Even when He has to be firm like a loving Father, He does it not through control but by giving us options. He presents us with a choice. And for the heart that truly knows His goodness, the choice is simple. His kindness really does lead us to repentance (Romans 2:4).

We established earlier in this book that the missing ingredient in the religious spirit is love, and we have seen how that lack can show up in how we view people and interact with them, misrepresenting God by acting apart from His love. In John's gospel account, he often to refers to himself as "the disciple Jesus loved." This has always struck me as humorous that John would self-identify this way because his unintended (or perhaps intended) inference is that He was Jesus' favorite in the bunch. However, I also love the insight he gives us into his own heart. He truly believed that Jesus loved him. It wasn't just a warm and fuzzy thought. It defined him.

John's identity was wrapped in the love of Jesus, which informed how he lived and loved others. Later in life, he would write these words: There is no fear in love. But perfect love drives out fear, because fear has to do with punishment. "The one who fears is not made perfect in love" (1 John 4:18). Love and fear cannot coexist.

When I first began to grasp this concept, it changed how I saw everything! I began to see the stranglehold fear had on me and how it harmed my connection with others. Fear fueled the anxiety that plagued me for years.

Love is not simply an idea. Love is expressed. It must look like something. Likewise, fear is expressed, and the evidence of fear is apparent if we only examine ourselves, our relationships, and our decisions. The startling truth is that most of us are riddled with it. It controls us. That's what fear does. Therefore, our longing for a sense of control stems from deep-seated fears. Whether it is fear of the future, financial instability, our kids' futures, abandonment, or rejection, the root of many fears is a lack of trust in God's provision, protection, love, and care for us.

So, naturally, when we're not trusting God, we try to control our circumstances. Unfortunately, when we fear people, we try to control them. And the most scared people are often the scariest people! Again, it is because love is missing from the equation. Fear is controlling us in the first place because we've lost sight of love — the love of God over us and, subsequently, our love for others. Where there is no love, fear will reign. And where fear reigns, a desire to control will consume us.

THE TYRANNY OF CONTROL

Chances are, we have all known controlling people. And, if we're honest, we have tried to control people at one time or another. Some traits of a controlling person are pretty obvious. For example, a controlling person might exude an air of infallibility, hold tightly to their ideas, and love being right. The "my way or the highway" attitude is a telling sign, as is a refusal to allow others to voice their opinions. (If they do, the controller certainly doesn't listen or accept others' points of view.) This stems from an inner insecurity that cannot cope with being wrong.

Controlling people are critical. Nothing or no one can be "good enough" for them, and they often blame-shift so they can keep up the facade that they have it all together. They project their insecurities onto others, attempting to control outcomes through manipulation.

Control doesn't just affect relationships. Control can also have disastrous effects when it is systematized and adopted into a culture. The most heinous acts in human history were made possible through organized control. Heinrich Heine, a German poet of Jewish origin who lived during the early 1800s, penned these words after watching his fellow countrymen show their patriotism by tossing "un-German" books into bonfires: "Where they burn books, they will also ultimately burn people."

He wrote this haunting prophecy long before the horrific events of the Holocaust and World War II, during which 11 million people perished. Control has dangerous implications. And it isn't confined to dictators or governments. No, it hits a little closer to home.

Religion, at its core, is antithetical to love. Therefore, it seeks to control. That's why those religious leaders who operated under its influence tried to kill Jesus. The religious spirit will flatter you until it can't control you. Then, when it can no longer control you, it will crucify you. Control is unmistakable evidence of the religious spirit.

You don't need to look far into Church history to see the controlling nature of the institution of the Church. Don't misunderstand my motive or heart here. I love the Church. I have answered God's call to serve the Church for the rest of my life. And I'm a member of it! But no one can argue that we've had a squeaky-clean past...or present.

The dark history of control and manipulation in the Church should cause us to examine our motives and methods. We will look further into Church history in a later chapter. For now, I'll simply state that the religious spirit is painfully apparent in how the Church has operated throughout the centuries.

In many ways, fear and control have become our status quo. Sadly, it's often the only way of Christian living we've been exposed to. But there is another way to live; it looks more like Jesus than a dragon.

I'm going to say something that should be obvious to us all. Jesus is not controlling. Now, that sounds like a no-brainer, right? But does the Church reflect that image of Jesus? Maybe a better question is, "Do we believe that?" Do we know Jesus as a tyrant or a shepherd?

Scripture paints a picture of God as a loving, compassionate Father who is patient in guiding His children even in their unbelief. Even in His anger toward their hard-heartedness, He gives them many chances to come to Him and be led. David said, "Do not be like the horse or the mule, which have no understanding but must be controlled by bit and bridle or they will not come to you" (Psalm 32:9 NIV).

Only stubborn horses and mules must be controlled. The heart of the Father is not that He would have to lead us with "bit and bridle" but that we would freely come to Him and receive Him as the Good Shepherd. His "rod and staff" that comfort offer the best way (Psalm 23). Even in our rebellion, He doesn't control us. Even when we disobey, argue with Him, blame Him, and curse Him, He leads us by calling us to Himself.

Close to Jesus is the best place to be. Nearness is the only way to live. His nearness corrects us and provides a center for us to recalibrate. Just as the children of Israel camped around His presence in the wilderness, we find our center in Him.

Don't misunderstand. Jesus certainly wasn't a pushover. He said what needed to be said and didn't hold back. He rebuked people often, especially His disciples, and He was savage with religious leaders. In our culture, I fear we have confused niceness with kindness. Jesus was always kind. But He wasn't restricted by niceness. On one occasion, when His disciples couldn't cast a demon out of a boy who was being severely tormented, Jesus sounded like He'd had enough of everyone's unbelief: "You unbelieving generation," Jesus replied, "How long shall I stay with you? How long shall I put up with you? Bring the boy to me" (Mark 9:19 NIV).

When the boy's father also admitted that He was struggling with his faith that Jesus could heal the boy, Jesus answered, "Everything is possible for one who believes" (verse 23). And what did He do? He certainly didn't exercise punishment for everyone's lack of faith and withhold freedom for this boy.

Instead, he expelled the demon, lifted the boy off the ground, and sent him on his way totally free. Not only did He heal the kid, but He also instructed the disciples on how to succeed next time. The only control Jesus exercised was over the demonic. I see His heart in this. Don't get tripped up on His passion and miss His heart. He was so passionate because He loved so much. But He never forced anyone to do what He asked. His commands always came with the option to obey or disobey. If Jesus didn't seem to feel the need to control people, neither should we. If Jesus didn't punish people for their unbelief or shortcomings, neither should we.

FEAR FACTORY

One of the most common ways that the Church operates in the area of control and fear is how we present the gospel to people. When I was a teenager, every October, we would load the church van (shoutout to all my 90s youth group crowd) and attend the equivalent of a "Christian haunted house." Although these events differed in theme from year to year, the general idea was to set up various rooms where different scripts would be acted out. Small groups would be led from room to room, following the story of two or more people who were presented with the gospel message. In the act, one of the main characters ultimately prayed to receive Jesus and "get saved," while the other rejected Christ.

What followed was a trip through two different rooms that graphically illustrated each character's eternal destination. So in the scene following the main character's death, the group experienced the fate of the person who didn't choose the right path. And if you've been to one of these events before, you know what this room was called. You guessed it! The "Hell Room."

Intense heat smacked you in the face as the doors opened. The room was almost entirely dark, with space heaters to make it feel as close to Hell as possible. The experience was immersive; people would run up to you screaming and crying, begging you to help them. Sometimes "the Devil" would also come out, scare the ever-living daylights out of everyone, and give 12-year-olds nightmares for years to come.

I know I'm being dramatic here. But you had to have been through one of these things as a preteen to understand! Once all the screaming and sweating were over, the group would be led into the (pleasantly air-conditioned) "Heaven Room," where our main character, who made the right choice, was greeted and embraced by Jesus. This part always moved me, especially after making it out of "Hell." In the end, someone would typically come out and give a presentation of the gospel message and allow those in the room who weren't "100% positive" about where they would go if they died to raise their hands and repeat a prayer to ask Jesus into their hearts. And who wouldn't want to do that, right? Especially after getting the crap scared out of them!

I'm being sarcastic, but I want to be clear. It's possible there were many genuine conversions as people heard the gospel and believed in Jesus for their salvation as a result. I'm sure this type of event was a door for many to truly receive Jesus as Savior. But I've also witnessed countless teenagers raise their hands and say a prayer out of coercion and fear, teenagers who didn't meet the real Jesus, and it shows.

Scores of people in the Church "make a decision" but never become disciples. The more I attended these events, the more I walked away with a weird feeling. Once I became a youth pastor, I even took a group of teenagers to one of these events. On the way home that night, I thought, "What kind of 'good news' is this if we have to scare people into believing it?"

Is the gospel about deciding where to spend eternity? Or is the gospel about having a life-changing encounter with Jesus that convinces us to become His disciple? What do we "believe" in when we pray out of fear of judgment? I know that judgment is a reality. Jesus Himself talked about Hell a lot. But I don't see Jesus even coming close to manipulating anyone into a "decision" for Him.

Instead, I see Jesus calling people to believe and follow Him. And then He leaves the ball in their court. Even if you're reading this from a reformed position theologically, and you interpret Scripture through a lens of "irresistible grace," that's not the same thing as "manipulative grace." Jesus never has and never will control people. Instead, He patiently and passionately calls us to Himself, drawing us close by His Holy Spirit. It's not His goal to force anyone into compliance. But that's what religion does. And unfortunately, that's what well-meaning people have done in His name.

My haunted house story is an over-the-top example of how we can let our methods taint good motives if we're not cautious. We can even slip into manipulating people into making that decision based on fear and not from a genuine place of repentance in response to the beauty of Jesus and His gospel. They miss that it's really good news. Manipulation can be subtle. It is possible to even operate in our gifting while operating in manipulation.

SPIRITUAL COERCION

Having studied the Scriptures for years, I'm convinced that the gifts of the Holy Spirit are in operation today — all of them. I didn't always believe that. But taking the Bible at face value and beginning to experience the things about which I read changed my mind over time.

I'll give an example concerning the gift of prophecy. It is beautiful and needed in the Church. God has used this gift to change my life, confirm His will, and rescue me from pits of despair, all with a word from Him through a brother or sister in Christ. I love this gift because it beautifully demonstrates the Father's heart toward us. But, like I said, I didn't always believe in it. I had seen what I perceived as weirdness and spiritual abuse around the subject, so I didn't want anything to do with it. Over time, I became more open to it, but I couldn't say I'd ever seen it in real life.

I remember the first time I experienced the gift of prophecy firsthand. I was a youth pastor and had taken my students to a conference in our city. After one of the sessions, another youth pastor who was helping lead it called me over to pray with a young man who was a junior in high school. The other youth pastor was female, so I assumed she wanted me to come over and pray with them so a male leader would also be present. I obliged and placed my hand on the young man's shoulder as she began to pray for him. There was nothing unusual about her prayer until she got several sentences in. Then, something changed. Instead of talking to God, she shifted her language. "I feel like God is saying..." she began.

What followed was incredible. As she revealed specifics in her prayer, thoughts the young man was thinking, what his father had recently said to him, and a few other facts about his future (none of which she could have known), he began to weep.

He was a popular kid, a junior in high school, a baseball player, and here he was weeping in front of his peers, in the presence of God, undone by the Father's specificity and intentionality. As I stood there with my hand still on his shoulder, I was undone as well. Shocked is a better word. I remember thinking as the light bulb switched on: "This is prophecy. I'm seeing the Biblical gift of prophecy right now!" It was beautiful. That moment set me on a course to discover just how beautiful the Holy Spirit and His gifts could be.

I've seen not only the good but also the bad and the ugly in the prophetic. Just because there is misuse or abuse doesn't mean we should reject it altogether. Take teaching, for example. Plenty of misuse and abuse have occurred in teaching, but we don't throw out teaching. We just bring correction.

It should be the same with the prophetic gifts. Unfortunately, the gift of prophecy has been the source of hurt and pain for some. Why? How could prophecy, such a precious gift from the Spirit, be harmful?

The answer is control. When prophecy is used to manipulate people, and it certainly has been, it cheapens the value of the gift in the eyes of others who experience pain and disillusionment from it. People have given me a "word from God" that included a directive to do exactly as they told me. Of course, I'm paraphrasing, but that was the tone of the prophecy.

The idea that someone can hear a special message from God from someone else is Biblical. However, the idea that they cannot be questioned is not. Anytime someone claims to have a "word" for you, especially directing you to do something in response to that word but refuses to be held accountable for the word they give, just don't go there. Instead, say thanks and move along. Do not fall into a paralyzing trap of fear just because someone claims to hear from God for you. Instead, you walk with God and let God confirm others' words in your own life.

So, the warning is: don't let prophecy become something God never intended it to become. As a child of God and follower of Jesus, you can hear God for yourself. Jesus said, "My sheep hear my voice, and I know them, and they follow me" (John 10:27 NIV). Don't wait on someone else to bring the word of the Lord to you. Ask Him yourself. He still talks to His kids.

Paul also warns us against rejecting His words. He says, "Do not quench the Spirit. Do not despise prophecies, but test everything; hold fast what is good" (1 Thessalonians 5:19-21 ESV). It's pretty straightforward. Do not despise prophecies. Depending upon our experiences with prophecy, that might be difficult. But I love how an older lady in our church put it once. She said, "If someone tells me something I'm unsure about, I don't throw it out. I sit it up on the 'shelf' and let it stay there. Then, one day, I might see that old word on the 'shelf,' and God might have something to say about it." That sounds like wisdom to me!

For those of us who love the prophetic, it would suit us well to deliver the word of the Lord and trust Him to work instead of trying to force someone to receive the word or force something to happen. What if we just trusted God? Novel concept. But that is the essential issue with control. It is not only a lack of love. It is a lack of trust.

As a pastor, I have had to learn a good lesson in communicating the Bible's truths. I'm still learning and growing, but I've come a long way in love. In my early years of ministry, I was under the impression that

I always had to be confrontational when preaching. I didn't see the people in the chairs (or pews then) as people who actually wanted to do what God said. I had probably taken my cues from preachers I'd heard before and didn't know any better. But it never felt right to me. Deep down, I knew it wasn't who I was. It was a facade. I thought that's what God wanted from me. I thought that's what "really good preaching" was supposed to be like. Don't get me wrong; preaching must confront our preconceived notions, callousness toward God, and complacency in our walk with Him. Sometimes we need a "hard" word to shake us out of our slumber. But to assume the worst about the people I'm communicating with is unfair, at best, and flat-out wrong if I'm doing it void of love.

I'll never forget the timely advice from a seasoned pastor that changed my perspective. He said, "When you preach to God's people, you preach to those who have been given new hearts." That revelation changed me as a preacher and leader.

Suddenly it became clear that I was carrying a false responsibility of changing people, and I wasn't trusting God to do His work in their lives. Leaving the results to God frees me to be myself. This has been an ongoing work of the Holy Spirit in my life, and I'm looking forward to the more profound work that He will do in me as I continue to walk with Him. I can honestly say that today, I love being a pastor. I love doing what God has called me to do. What changed? My need to control.

Control is a trademark of the religious spirit. It was present in the heart of the religious leaders when they sought to take Jesus out and later His disciples. Jesus' words would prove true after He was gone:

> If the world hates you, keep in mind that it hated me first. If you belonged to the world, it would love you as its own. As it is, you do not belong to the world, but I have chosen you out of the world. That is why the world hates you.
>
> JOHN 15:18-19 NIV

Post-Pentecost, the apostles were under the same scrutiny their Rabbi had endured. In one instance, they were brought before the Sanhedrin, the Jewish supreme council. The high priest questioned Peter and the other apostles about why they continued to teach their "false religion." They responded, "We must obey God rather than men" (Acts 5:29 ESV). As expected, the religious leaders didn't like that response at all! They were so angry, they tried to kill them on the spot.

> But before their rage-filled wishes could be fulfilled, Gamaliel, one of the most respected men in the Sanhedrin, intervened. He addressed his fellow council members after having the apostles escorted out of the chamber. He warned his peers to be careful about how they handled these rebels, reminding them that this wasn't the first time this had happened. There had been other leaders who gained followers and challenged the authority of the ruling religious system, and every time this happened, it fizzled out, becoming nothing. Then he charged them, "So in the present case I tell you, keep away from these men and let them alone, for if this plan or this undertaking is of man, it will fail; but if it is of God, you will not be able to overthrow them. You might even be found opposing God!"
>
> ACTS 5:38-39 ESV

Wisdom found its way into the most religious spot in Jerusalem that day. They soon let the men go, and of course, they kept preaching about Jesus. Yet, Gamaliel's advice to the rest of the council is good for us when we find ourselves offended and slipping into control. Why not let God handle it? By doing so, we can avoid inadvertently opposing God's work and confidently rely on His providence. When our hands are off, it shows that we believe His hands are trustworthy.

CHAPTER EIGHT

Offense Over Humility

Travel with me to a moment in a convention center in downtown Nashville. I was an apprehensive conference attendee, an observer more than anything.

As soon as I walked into the sprawling room where the first session would take place, I was so uncomfortable. So nervous. I came here to check out what God was doing, and my heart was to know Him deeply. Was there something I didn't know, something I was missing out on? The hunger to learn more about Him led me to the event. I had no idea what I would experience, but I knew I would not be the same when I left, good or bad.

As the session kicked off, the worship that began to flow in that room was like nothing I had ever seen. It was wild, noisy, and chaotic for where I was then (compared to where I am now). Honestly, I was offended.

I then remembered a conversation I had with a friend. After reading a book about getting to know the Holy Spirit, he was offended because the book made him feel like he had not experienced everything about God there was to experience. My friend was offended at the thought of missing out on something, yet not hungry enough to find out what was available on the other side of offense.

This is a shared experience among people who have known Jesus for a long time but haven't considered there could be a more profound experience with Him than previously thought. I was stuck in that religious mindset as I observed people all around me shouting, dancing, swaying, twirling, bowing, and laying prostrate on the concrete floor. I didn't know how to think about what I was witnessing. I began to examine the lyrics of the songs we were singing together. They honored Jesus. They were rich in theological depth, something my spiritual background taught me to look for. Okay, so that checked out. But what about the expression of worship? To me, it was "over the top." I couldn't seem to get past my offense.

In this respect, an offense challenges our preconceived notions, traditions, and sensibilities. We are often offended when confronted with something beyond our experience, mainly because we never admit we need more. For a person who is seeking God, unable to quench the deep longing for more of Him, this hunger is the very thing that exposes them to offense. That was why I was in that room in the first place. If we could ever come to terms with our shortsightedness — that we don't have a corner on the truth — we might break through into something wonderful and essential for moving on in our relationship with Jesus.

Humility enables us to receive what we currently do not possess. This hurdle is not meant to jump over. The only way to get around offense is to go low, to humble yourself. Don't try to go around it. Don't try to dismiss it. Don't try to lift yourself over it. That's all a manifestation of pride. Humility is the only response to offense that will enable us to overcome it and move from glory to glory.

Offense is a red flag that signals we're about to slip into fear and control. It reeks of dragon. How do you respond when you are offended? The human response to offense varies widely.

ANGER AND DEFENSIVENESS

When offended, some people may react with immediate anger and defensiveness. They might feel attacked or threatened by the unfamiliar concept or idea and lash out in a verbal attack, or worse. This response is often driven by a fear of the unknown or insecurity. Let's be honest. It's tough to admit we are wrong, especially if we've long believed it. This level of offense can cause us to defend ourselves at all costs. It's not hard to spot in others, of course. Look no further than social media comment sections. But it's a little more challenging to notice in our own thinking.

A helpful practice to recognize our defensive reactions is to stop before we speak or act and simply ask ourselves, "Why am I angry right now?" Examining the source of our frustrations often reveals something more profound if we choose to see it. Letting emotions rule us is a sure way to lose any argument, if the goal is civility. And going with our gut reaction to defend our viewpoints without stopping to examine our thoughts further solidifies our wrong thinking because once we've lashed out in defense, it's no longer about the facts as much as it is about saving face.

Both sides lose when they are committed to justifying their beliefs without examining them honestly. But what if it's not really about winning an argument in the first place? As painful as it is, I've found that being confronted with my own error has often been the best thing for me. And it has always led to a measure of freedom of which I was not previously aware. It's been said that knowledge is power. Likewise, ignorance is a prison. But its prisoners don't know they're bound. The freedom of new ways of thinking cannot be experienced until the door has been opened. Pride is the lock. Humility is the key.

DISMISSAL OR DISINTEREST

Others may dismiss or ignore what they don't understand. They might downplay the topic's significance or avoid engaging with it altogether. This response can stem from a lack of curiosity, apathy, or an unwillingness to challenge their existing beliefs or comfort zone. After all, it's much easier to live in denial than to do the hard work of exploration and eventual demolition of some of our faulty beliefs.

For many years as a Christian, I avoided some challenging subjects simply because I didn't think they could be understood. But hunger does strange things to your will. Natural hunger will make someone search for food, and even beg for it. I've seen people dig through dumpster trash, looking for something to eat! My point is that spiritual hunger will move you to seek out what you don't have or don't know. When your appetite surpasses your apathy, things will get really interesting! An adventure awaits you on the other side of the choice to not settle for what you currently know.

There may be sections in this book that give you a reason to pause. If some of my statements cause you to be offended or upset, consider that an invitation to a deeper look into those topics or ideas. Who knows? You might learn something new. Or you might become more solidified in your own beliefs. Either way, you've worked to challenge your convictions and pursue truth, and that's a really good thing!

CURIOSITY AND OPENNESS

Some people, when offended, respond with genuine interest and a willingness to learn. They may recognize their need for greater understanding as an opportunity for growth, actively seek more information, or engage in dialogue to expand their knowledge. They may respond by seeking clarification or asking questions to gain understanding. They approach the situation with humility, acknowledge their lack, and express a genuine desire to learn more. This response can lead to productive conversations and bridge the gap between misunderstanding and comprehension.

That's what happened to me in my spiritual journey more times than I count now. I know I still don't have a corner on truth, I don't have all the answers, and I'm pretty sure I'm flat wrong about some things, but I've grown tremendously by breaking through my offense at the unknown and pursuing the whole truth...and the experience that comes with it. Authors and other influential people in my life challenged how

I thought. They stirred my hunger. I'm so thankful for the voices that guided me to a more profound understanding and experience.

It's essential to examine our feelings and beliefs when confronted with something we don't understand, to take a step back to evaluate our initial emotional response and consider whether the offense is justified or stems from personal biases or prejudices. This response requires introspection and self-awareness. And that requires humility—lots of it.

I am confident that this book will become a bridge for hungry people. Don't stop if you are challenged by what you're reading! Ask the Holy Spirit to guide you into truth. He's promised to do it. One of His primary activities in our lives is to lead us. So, submit your mind and heart to the Shepherd. He's a good one.

In that room with all the "crazy" stuff, I fought the urge to become dismissive or critical. I decided (with the help of the Holy Spirit) to go low and find Jesus on the other side of my offense. And I found Him. I had told Him, "I want all you have for me. Nothing more. Nothing less." I trusted Him to guide me past all the things I didn't understand, wasn't ready for, and straight to His heart. I was awakened that day to a whole new dimension of knowing the Father, Son, and Holy Spirit. Years later, the fruit is still good. I love Him more than ever. I'm so glad He was patient enough to lead me into deeper waters.

Are you longing for more? Do you wonder if you're living the life Jesus died (and raised) for you to live? Why not press through what you don't understand and let your offense drive you to experience more of Jesus than you ever thought possible? He's worth it.

If you have made it this far in the book, you are still interested or have sensed a holy whisper to keep reading. Let me just say thank you for sticking with it! You have done a marvelous job, and my prayer is that your mindsets are shifting and you are becoming more aware of the sway that religion can have over people. More importantly, I pray that you are being drawn into an awareness of the goodness of God and a better way to live — the Kingdom way.

We should stop here and do a little inward work. If you don't mind, take a moment and ask yourself the questions below. Be as honest as you can with your answers. Avoid the temptation to rush through this part. Instead, ask the Holy Spirit to reveal the truth as you work through them.

**SIT WITH THESE QUESTIONS LONG ENOUGH
FOR A DIVINE CONVERSATION TO BEGIN.**

» Is there any area of your life where you are exalting law over love?

» Are you more concerned about being right than showing love?

» Do the people who know you best see you as a "law person" or a "love person?"

» Do you ever feel more important or more "spiritual" than others because of what you know about the Bible?

» Have you known Jesus personally, or do you just know about Him?

» Do you love Christianity or church more than you love Jesus Himself?

» If some of the traditions you hold dear were removed from your faith practice, would you still be able to connect with God on a heart level?

» Do you have friends who are not believers in Jesus?

» Are people who don't believe in Jesus attracted to your life?

» What are you currently trying to control instead of trusting God?

» Do you believe the best about people or the worst?

Good job. Did you detect dragon-like attitudes or mindsets as you worked through those questions? If so, don't move on until you have acknowledged evidence of the religious spirit in your life. Confess and repent of whatever the Holy Spirit revealed to you. Then, go ahead and shut the door on the dragon.

Taking back your life from religion doesn't happen instantly, but moments like this draw a line in the sand and give us options to choose what voice we will allow to direct our lives moving forward. Don't be surprised if you start recognizing the subtle charm of the religious spirit when it starts to creep into your thoughts or language. Now that you realize the dragon's presence, you can resist it and embrace the way of Jesus instead.

CHAPTER NINE
Dragon Legends

Inventions sometimes go awry. The original intention for which something was created can get twisted into something altogether sinister. For example, Gerhard Schrader, a 33-year-old German chemist, was tasked by his government to develop a pesticide to protect the nation's crops to reduce dependency on imports. He hoped to make discoveries that would greatly aid the world hunger problem. Instead, he accidentally discovered what would later be developed and known as Sarin nerve agent, a brutal tool of chemical warfare. To witness your invention become an instrument of destruction must be devastating.

In many ways, the Church has become a shadow of what God originally intended. The consequences of our rejection of His design are dire. History is replete with examples of how the religious spirit has hijacked the Church and caused irreparable damage to people in the name of God. As uncomfortable as it is to acknowledge this fact, we must confront what has occurred. Undeniably, God's heart is grieved over it, yet He remains committed to forming His Church into a people who look like Him. We, too, must not run from the discomfort but rather face it head-on if we are to move forward in a better way.

Listen to the anguish in the words of a grieving Messiah over a people who chose to go their own way. "O Jerusalem, Jerusalem, the city that kills the prophets and stones God's messengers! How often I have wanted to gather your children together as a hen protects her chicks beneath her wings, but you wouldn't let me. And now, look, your house is abandoned and desolate." (Matthew 23:37-38 NLT)

The verses that follow this passage reveal that Jesus was standing in the shadow of the Temple while pronouncing its disastrous fate. At that moment, He was surrounded by a group of angry Pharisees (Matthew 22:41) who were blinded by religion to the truth and could not receive His words due to the hardness of their hearts. The backdrop of this confrontation, the awe-inspiring Temple, towered nearly 100 feet above them.

However, only Jesus saw the prophetic vision overlaying the natural like a hazy dream. He was foreseeing the destruction of that magnificent house of worship only forty years later. The Jewish revolt that would begin in 66 AD, and the subsequent Roman siege of Jerusalem in 70 AD, resulted in the destruction of the Temple and many thousands of the inhabitants of Jerusalem. This was not the only warning from Jesus concerning this event, and it was even predicted by the prophet Daniel hundreds of years prior (Luke 19:41-44; Luke 21:20-22; Daniel 9:26). Jesus also knew full well that "the city that kills the prophets and stones God's messengers" would soon be crying out, "Crucify Him!" Behind the people's blindness was a spirit at work. Care to guess which one? The same spirit that rejected the One who had come to save Israel is the same one that's alive and well today in the hearts of men and women who love religion more than God Himself.

The story began in a garden. A serpent convinced humanity that God was withholding something from them, and to become like God, they needed to take matters into their own hands. The enemy convinced them that eating from the tree of the knowledge of good and evil would be the key to having their eyes opened and being like God Himself. Adam and Eve both fell for it.

> When the woman saw that the fruit of the tree was good for food and pleasing to the eye, and also desirable for gaining wisdom, she took some and ate it. She also gave some to her husband, who was with her, and he ate it. Then the eyes of both of them were opened, and they realized they were naked; so

they sewed fig leaves together and made coverings for themselves.

GENESIS 3:6-7 NIV

This was when religion entered the picture, and Satan was its founder. He simply offered them another way to "become like God." They disregarded what God had said and believed the enemy's lie. Ironically, they were already like God, made in His image. But that's what religion does. It seeks to convince us of our need to be "good enough" or "right enough" to earn our stripes. It always proves futile, chasing what we already have instead of turning our gaze toward the One who can make us righteous.

Notice that their initial response to doing things their own way was shame. They hid. The religious spirit brings a lot of luggage with it, and shame is its carry-on. And we, imagers made to radiate the goodness and beauty of the Lord, are reduced to a dim glow, if not a smoldering wick, all because of shame. But the astounding thing about the gospel is that it calls us out of shame and beckons us to shine again, to reflect the glory of the Lord. Jesus makes way for us to be forgiven and return to our original purpose — to be radiant ones!

Arise, shine, for your light has come, and the glory of the LORD has risen upon you.

ISAIAH 60:1 ESV

You are the light of the world. A city set on a hill cannot be hidden. Nor do people light a lamp and put it under a basket, but on a stand, and it gives light to all in the house. In the same way, let your light shine before others, so that they may see your good works and give glory to your Father who is in Heaven.

MATTHEW 5:14-16 ESV

Jesus intends to burn bright within you, but religion will snuff you out if you let it! So many lights have been stamped out by the dragon's foot. Many more never found the flame. In perhaps the greatest tragedy in our history, the religious spirit stole the heart of humanity.

DIVIDING WALLS

Following Germany's defeat in World War II, the capital city of Berlin was divided into four sections. The U.S., British, and French would control the western regions of the city while Soviet Russia controlled the eastern side. Over time, these areas became part of East Germany and West Germany. They were divided by a wall, primarily to keep citizens of East Germany from defecting to the other side and finding freedom from the repressive Soviet Occupation Zone. The wall remained, separating the two countries, from 1961 to 1989.

President Ronald Reagan gave his famous speech there two years before its demolition, with that wall serving as a dramatic backdrop. In the speech, he called on Soviet leader, Mikhail Gorbachev, to "tear down this wall!" I was six years old when that wall came down. I can remember watching scenes on the news while thousands of Germans climbed the wall with pick axes and sledgehammers, tearing it down piece by piece. With the wall down, freedom and peace could finally be attainable.

Somewhere around 45,000 Christian denominations exist today. That's staggering, considering it all started with a handful of followers. It reveals the astounding numbers of people who follow the teachings of Jesus, but it also shows the sheer lack of unity among the global Church. Denominational distinctives range from differing beliefs around baptism, communion, styles of worship, and much more. It's mind-boggling.

I'm not one to say we shouldn't have distinctives and clear statements about what we believe concerning essential doctrines of the faith. But I sometimes wonder how our current state of disunity must differ wildly from how Jesus sees His Bride. Sometimes the Church looks more like the Bride of Frankenstein than the Bride of Christ! Seriously though, I wonder if what we consider normal, being separate, grieves His heart beyond what we can imagine. And it's not just the fact that we are divided within, but even more so, it's how the Church has treated those outside.

Sadly, Church history is replete with examples of how the religious spirit has operated freely yet deceptively in the institution that is supposed to foster freedom and love in the world around it. One doesn't have to look into the past very long for evidence of a dragon lurking in the Church. We have seen this exact scenario play out time and time again in its history. We have blasted people, maligning and accusing them of their inability to see the truth and live accordingly.

If you haven't noticed, the Church has a bad reputation with some sections of society for this reason. We are eager to shout our opinions and push our doctrines without compassion for the ones we are attacking. And this onslaught of religious fervor is not reserved for those outside the Church. The attack has been just as violent within the Church. We devour each other over doctrinal differences such as the end times, baptism, and musical and preaching styles. Division is rampant. I think it is normal for us to have differing viewpoints. After all, you can't have unity without disagreement. But when secondary issues become the reasons for maligning, dishonoring, and outright attacking those who disagree with us, we're probably being influenced by the dragon.

I don't see a God erecting walls to divide when I read the Bible. Instead, I see a God who delights in tearing those walls down. You might be saying, "Well, what about Jesus's claim He came not to bring peace but a sword in Matthew 10:34?"

Reading these words of Jesus in context reveals that He's talking about people either choosing to accept or reject Him. Jesus is not intentionally separating families here. Instead, He highlights the cost of following Him and presents a sobering reality that not all will choose that way. Because of this, a son might oppose his father, and a daughter turn against her mother because they ultimately choose separate paths when faced with the call to follow.

A line waits in the sand for those who would follow our Jewish Messiah. There's no way around it. Not everyone wants Him. As a river separates when it encounters an obstacle, naturally, humanity's free will necessitates division. Eventually, some of the water in the river will take another path, down a tributary perhaps, but you can be sure it will flow where it wills. That kind of division occurs in many instances — in nature, in relationships, and, as we see here, in a person's spiritual life. But the type of division that builds walls that Jesus never meant to build is the work of the religious spirit.

In chapter 2 of Ephesians, Paul gives a beautiful presentation of what the cross accomplished in the lives of believers:

> But because of his great love for us, God, who is rich in mercy, made us alive with Christ even when we were dead in transgressions—it is by grace you have been saved. And God raised us up with Christ and seated us with him in the heavenly realms in Christ Jesus, in order that in the coming ages He might show the incomparable riches of his grace, expressed in his kindness to us in Christ Jesus.
>
> EPHESIANS 2:4-7 NIV

Then he explains how, through Christ's blood, Jews and Gentiles are no longer two groups but one family. Speaking to the Gentile believers, he says:

> But now in Christ Jesus, you who once were far away have been brought near by the blood of Christ. For He himself is our peace, who has made the two groups one and has destroyed the barrier, the dividing wall of hostility, by setting aside in His flesh the law with its commands and regulations. His purpose was to create in Himself one new humanity out of the two, thus making peace, and in one body to reconcile both of them to God through the cross, by which He put to death their hostility. He came and preached peace to you who were far away and

peace to those who were near. For through Him we both have access to the Father by one Spirit.

EPHESIANS 2:13-18 NIV

When Paul says that Jesus "set aside the law with its commands and regulations," this doesn't mean He put an end to the law. In Matthew's gospel, Jesus tells us plainly that's not what He did: "Do not think that I have come to abolish the Law or the Prophets; I have not come to abolish them but to fulfill them" (Matthew 5:17 NIV). What Paul is referring to in Ephesians 2 is not the law itself but rather the exhausting list of religious requirements added to the law. The Greek word for "regulations" in this passage is the word from which we derive "dogma." These types of regulations are not the commands of God. Instead, they are the dogmatic application of the commands. These don't set people free but rather enslave them again. There are many examples in Scripture of such additions and applications that build a wall, figuratively speaking, between God and people.

One literal example of a wall that God never erected was a feature of the Temple during the time of Jesus. He would have frequented the Second Temple (or Herod's Temple.) The Babylonians destroyed the original Temple of Solomon in 586 BC, and years later, a very modest new temple, known as Zerubbabel's Temple, would be constructed. The much more impressive structure would be built later by Herod the Great, beginning around 20 BC. This upgrade consisted of structural changes not included in God's instructions for making the original Temple. For example, in the Old Testament, the only wall separating anyone in the Temple was between the priests and the laity. This was the command in Scripture.

But later, walled courtyards that prevented women and Gentiles from coming any closer were added. While in the Court of the Gentiles, Jesus flipped the tables and drove out the money changers. This gives essential context to Jesus's rebuke when He says, "Is it not written: 'My house will be called a house of prayer for all nations'? But you have made it a den of robbers" (Mark 11:17 NIV). This statement tells us that God's intention for His house was never to keep anyone out but rather to welcome all.

I see the same old religious theme of men attempting to improve upon God's commands. Unfortunately, we erect walls God never intended, however zealous our intent. Unlike the Berlin Wall, these walls aren't made of cinder blocks and barbed wire. But walls of disagreement, differing beliefs, and preferences that the Church has erected throughout the centuries have made it hard (even impossible) for people to approach God. They have divided us from each other, as well.

STAINED GLASS CEILINGS

I can't move on from the topic of walls without addressing how religion has alienated women in particular. Christianity has done far more to value and empower women than any other religious system. Consider the major religions and observe how women are viewed in those contexts. In certain religious sects, women are not allowed to speak publicly or reveal any part of their bodies, even veiling their eyes. That sounds extreme, and it is.

But I don't have to tell you that Christianity also owns a history of treating women as inferior. We might not make our women wear burkas, but we silence them by referencing passages in our Bible that are taken out of context. Somehow we have viewed our suppression of women in the Church as a mark of doctrinal purity and faithfulness. Meanwhile, our sisters and daughters (over half of the Church) are told to sit in silence.

Have you ever considered why in Genesis chapter 3, the serpent tempts Eve first? I've heard it taught that Eve was an easy target, and "that's why we can't trust a woman's discernment." Really? It makes me wonder if the person teaching had ever met a woman!

Consider this. What if the serpent pursued the "real" threat first? Since the woman had been given a place of influence, wouldn't she be a perfect target? Womanhood has always been under attack because women are essential in the Kingdom plan. A look at world history reveals that the enemy must be terrified of children and women because he has tried to murder the innocent and oppress women from day one. The spirit of religion has often followed suit, placing women in a lower caste, like a problem to be solved.

Hear me. A woman is not a problem to solve but a problem solver to be valued and celebrated. The creation story affirms women. And why is creation so important? It gives us a glimpse at God's design—His intention—before sin tainted everything. In the beginning, woman's purpose was the same as man's: to know God and partner with Him to extend the Kingdom on Earth, to "co-rule." And that hasn't changed. I propose that the subjugation of women is a result of the religious spirit, not God's original design.

In total, 317 women or groups of women are mentioned in the Old Testament alone. Among those listed are some fantastic examples of influential leaders and mouthpieces for God: Sarah, Hagar, Miriam, Deborah, Hannah, Esther, and Huldah. The list continues. When we come to the New Testament, we see Jesus, the exact representation of God (Hebrews 1:3), treating women with honor, dignity, and respect, even sending them out as His messengers.

Mary Magdalene was the first person to tell the good news of the resurrection, and Jesus explicitly told her to do so! Upon seeing the promised Messiah as a baby, Anna, the prophetess, who had been in the Temple praying and fasting day and night, told everyone that He was the One (Luke 2:36-38). In Paul's letters to the churches in Asia and Rome, we find mention of women prophesying in gatherings (1 Corinthians 11), female house church leaders (Romans 16; Acts 28), deaconesses (Romans 16), and even a woman apostle (Romans 16), which meant she would have been a "sent one" or missionary, and possibly a church planter. Do you think she completed the task silently? Of course not.

The overarching narrative of the Bible gives a resounding "yes" to women. I'm aware of the debate in some circles surrounding women's roles in the Church. Again, most of these arguments stem from interpreting passages removed from their original cultural context.

Building a case for affirming women in the Church is not the purpose of this book, but I would encourage you to do some serious study on this topic, and I believe that you will come to see that Scripture, as a whole, gives more freedom to women than prohibitions.

If you are a woman reading this, I want you to step into the full purpose of God for your life. Don't let the dragon claim the treasure that you are. The enemy's desire to silence and sit you down is no coincidence. You are a threat to his kingdom. If you are a man reading this, especially in spiritual leadership, I implore you to empower the women in your environments and make space for their voices. Let their perspectives add wisdom to the conversation. Invite women to the table. By doing so, you may be advancing the Kingdom of God more than you realize. In its fullest expression, the Church, male, and female, as imagers of God together, is the world's hope.

I am no wrecking ball. I love the Church. I value its traditions and its contributions to the world. But some of our walls are meant to fall. I see a rising generation of believers who aren't afraid to boldly call for walls to come down in Jesus' name, pick up their sledgehammers, and get to work. May we be wise in our demolition, having the same fervor to build as we do to tear down.

CHAPTER TEN
Destructive Intent

A few years ago, I walked through one of the most challenging seasons of ministry I've experienced. It was a very confusing time. Day after day, a persistent fog clouded my thinking, and the voice of the Lord I had known to be so apparent at other times in my life seemed strangely silent. At that time, I questioned my calling, my ability to lead the church, and even my identity as God's child. When I tried to be still, intrusive thoughts bombarded my mind and heart in an anxious swirl.

I felt unsure of everything. That's not an exaggeration. The pandemic interrupted our lives, hurling leaders (including me) into an unusually complex predicament. While the stresses of the rapidly changing culture weighed on me and the constant pressure to make decisions affecting the people in my care, part of the problem was my own. I gave too much weight to too many voices. I took in too much noise.

Don't get me wrong. There is value in counsel. I believe in listening to the input of people who have walked the road before me. But when any other voices replace the voice of the Lord in your life, you stay lost. No one can replace your connection to His heart and His voice, no matter their position in the Church or their level of gifting. We are inundated with opinions through media outlets. Social media has given everyone a voice. Unfortunately, it opens us up to more influence and noise than we bargain for.

A deluge of politically charged, manipulative advice came to me from all directions. Most of the time, I could discern through the fog. But the most challenging part was discerning what sounded spiritual but had a religious underpinning. It is possible to shroud our preferences in religious language to make it more justifiable to ourselves or convince others we are right.

We have all done it at some point. Throw in a "God told me," and all truth is up for grabs. This was happening almost daily for many of us in the Church. The messaging from government leaders and the Church seemed to conflict. It was confusing, from wearing to not wearing masks, and how the church should be run. Was I hearing God's voice? Did I even know His voice?

Honestly, I didn't know what to do with all of this. It was like a spiritual tug-of-war, and it was, in a real sense, paralyzing for me. It had me feeling stuck as a leader and in my walk with God.

One night during that season of confusion, I had a dream. In it, I was surrounded by an angry mob closing in on me. As they approached, I noticed how they all had something in common in how they dressed. The men closest to me all wore some form of religious attire. One was dressed like a priest, one like a rabbi, and another as an imam. In the dream, I knew that these individuals represented religion. As my focus turned to their faces, I looked into their eyes, and the only way to describe what I saw was unbridled rage. These people didn't just want to catch me. They wanted me dead. I woke up just as they were grabbing me.

To this day, it was the worst nightmare I've ever had. It scared me so badly that I sat straight up in bed and cried out in fear. This woke my wife and had the same effect on her! I was immediately hit with the realization that what I was facing in that season was none other than the religious spirit. I had not recognized it in the people speaking into my life. But more importantly, I had not realized its presence in my life.

The spirit of religion is a deeply rooted mindset that can influence us in ways we don't realize. The real enemy had been exposed through that dream and was certainly not a timid foe. It became clear to me almost instantly that I could no longer afford to tolerate its influence in my life. The religious spirit is not passive. It is set on destruction. Therefore, it must be dealt with.

The spirit of religion must be broken. It takes a violent oppositional force to kill it. So in the following weeks, I had to take a serious inventory of my heart and mind, asking the Lord to search me and root out any religion in me that I was allowing to stay. I also had to take inventory of the voices I was allowing to influence my thinking in that season of my life. Religion doesn't leave quietly. It must be cut off.

I want to remind you that killing the dragon is not about targeting people in a witch hunt. You probably don't know if the religious mindset is influencing you. But the same is true of those influencing you in that same spirit. They do not realize they are falling prey to its subtleties. So be sure to extend abundant grace to people trying to control or manipulate you in the name of God. A spirit is at work that they don't see. Silence, not retaliation, is the best weapon against accusation and manipulation.

Listen. Be ruthless with the religious spirit in your own life. Don't allow the dragon to stay where he does not belong one more day. He is guarding a treasure that isn't his. The sooner you kill him, the sooner you can claim what is rightfully yours as a joint heir with Jesus.

SACRED TALES AND DRAGON SCALES

I love history — ancient, church, revival, and war history. I like it all. One thing I love about history is that it's honest. If the historian has done his job, there will inevitably be parts of history that we would rather sweep under the rug and forget ever happened.

It's honest, brutally honest. It's sometimes more complex than we want. Life is complicated, and so is history. Even our most celebrated histories have their inconvenient truths. In 1945, the world celebrated the surrender of Germany and, later, Japan, bringing the Second World War to a welcomed end. But as the ticker tape flew above American cities and radio announcers heralded the news of peace, the fact remained that freedom was bought at an incredible price.

An estimated 40-50 million people died during World War II. The first and only use of atomic warfare by the United States against the Japanese Empire decimated two cities and killed between 129,000 and 226,000 people, most of whom were civilians. This is a problematic tension, isn't it? Nevertheless, history often exposes our consciences to an unsettling tension that can teach us valuable lessons if we embrace it.

The same is valid with the history of Christianity. It is tempting to avoid the sordid past and omit details that don't help our case. After all, arguments against the faith often include the atrocities done in the name of Christ. Whether it was the Crusades, the Protestant Inquisition, or the modern-day abuses found among those who claim the name "Christian," there is no denying that we have a regrettable past.

But how can it be that a religion whose two primary tenants are "love God" and "love your neighbor as yourself" is capable of producing such a history of violence and suffering? As Blaise Pascal once said, "Men never do evil so completely and cheerfully as when they do it from religious conviction." To truly understand Church history, you can't ignore the presence of the religious spirit within its pages.

Let's begin an uncomfortable look into the past, beginning with the Crusades. For 200 years, crusaders traveled from Western Europe under the banner of a "Holy War" to expel Muslims from the Holy Land, reclaiming Jerusalem and the surrounding area for the Kingdom of God. The First Crusade, proclaimed by Pope Urban II in November of 1095, inaugurated a time of great suffering that became an indelible stain on the reputation of the Church for centuries. For Pope Urban and the other popes who ruled during the Crusades, the military action against the "infidels" was vindication. To them, it was about justice.

The principles of "just war," laid out by Augustine hundreds of years prior, called for respect for hostages, prisoners, and civilians. But in the heat of this Holy War, there seemed to be a total disregard for this code, and innocent people endured unspeakable atrocities at the hands of the "defenders of the faith" on their religious escapade. It's been said that the road to Hell is paved with good intentions. Unfortunately, that statement holds a lot of truth. I don't think anyone sets out to damage the cause of Christ. But I believe that people with the best intentions can actually cause the most damage, especially when religious zeal is the engine that fuels it.

The Crusades were not the only embarrassment in the history of Christendom. While the crusaders' enemies were of another faith, the Inquisition of the 12th century focused on heretics within the institution itself. Heresy is "the act of having an opinion or belief that is the opposite of or against what is the official or popular opinion." In our modern-day, Western, individualized version of faith, it is hard for us to imagine a Medieval view of heresy. But the Medieval Christians would never consider one's faith a private matter as we often do, nor would they consider it a matter of secondary importance.

The eternal consequences of one's actions were at the forefront of the Medieval mind, not to mention how one's beliefs affected the whole religious community, especially if a minority challenged long-standing beliefs. Nothing happened in a spiritual vacuum. Faith, and how it was expressed, carried weight within the larger Church context.

Nowadays, among Christian bloggers and YouTube critics, the term "heretic" is thrown around far too loosely. The slightest difference in secondary or tertiary matters can get one labeled a heretic in today's online community. But while the cost of such an accusation today amounts to your name being dragged through the mud or accused in the comment section, things were a tad more severe in the Medieval era. Thus, from the viewpoint of the established institution, the Inquisition was a necessary safeguard to maintain a peaceful society.

Can you spot those good intentions? Not only were accused heretics executed, but they were also often tortured using the most inhumane methods imaginable. This was meant to discourage questioning of the powers that be, quell heretical beliefs, and maintain the purity of the Church. If you were a Medieval Christian who dared challenge the authority of the Church or question any of its beliefs or practices, you would be lucky if the only thing that happened to you was the refusal to baptize your kids or forbidding you to partake in communion.

At the more extreme end of punishment, you could be burned at the stake or dismembered. Yikes. Those online comments don't sting so much in comparison, do they? The truth is that many of our brothers and sisters in the faith were martyred because they were committed to remaining faithful to Jesus and His Word.

Peter Waldo, the leader of the Waldenses, launched a mission to the poor and translated sections of the Bible into French to bring the good news to those without access to it. He taught them the Scriptures and sent others to do the same. Someone like Waldo would receive a "church member of the year" award today. But the Inquisition came to his doorstep with divorce papers, as it were, and he was excommunicated. His crime? Preaching the gospel without permission from the ruling bishops. This further encouraged his followers to regard the commands of Scripture rather than the Pope and other church leaders. Choosing to obey God rather than men meant they would flee persecution for most of their lives.

Around this time, the rumblings of the Reformation were being felt all over Europe. Voices began to rise like never before in response to the abuses of the papacy. "Christ alone is the head of the Church," said the zealot John Wycliffe. Likewise, the Czech reformer John Huss would not bow to the fear of death. When pressured to confess and renounce his errors or be burned, he wrote: "I have said that I would not, for a chapel full of gold, recede from the truth."

By the time of the Protestant Reformation (1517-1648), a groundswell of religious persecution was in full swing. In Zurich, Switzerland, the reformation led by Ulrich Zwingli (1484-1531) challenged the religious institution of baptism. As a result, he and his followers became known as the Anabaptists. But, as they studied the Scriptures, they concluded that new believers should be baptized when converted, so they ignored custom and continued the practice known today as "believers' baptism."

As people believed in the gospel of grace, the new converts were baptized in water. In response, the authorities in Zurich began rounding up newly baptized men and throwing them into jail. When this did little to sway the Anabaptists' convictions, the Zurich council finally gave them what they wanted. The first martyr of the group, Felix Manz, drowned in the Limmat River on January 5, 1527. During the Reformation, nearly five thousand Anabaptists were executed by drowning, burning, and the sword.

With the Protestants' newfound religious freedom due to the Reformation, you would think they would have learned a thing or two about how to treat people with differing views. On the contrary, they were not innocent of the sins of their Catholic inquisitors. They would soon begin burning their own.

John Calvin (1509-1564) introduced theological concepts to the Church that still influence how we interpret the Scriptures today. He gave us a sure theological foundation in God's sovereignty and man's depravity.

Today's evangelical Christianity finds its roots in the theological framework Calvin championed. Even though he found himself on the brink of exile for his teachings, he also silenced his theological opponents. A council was established in Calvin's city of Geneva, Switzerland, to address matters of church discipline in the community. At times, the council would pronounce judgment upon detractors and, with the local authorities' help, enact penalties incurred by challenging Calvin and his teachings. One such detractor was Jacques Gruet, who was arrested, tortured, and beheaded in 1547. His crime was writing a letter to John Calvin in which he called Calvin a "hypocrite." Gruet's house was later burned while his wife looked on helplessly.

The most well-known opponent of Calvin was Michael Servetus. He was dealt with similarly when he criticized Calvin's teachings. Calvin wrote of his intentions in a letter dated February 1546.

Servetus would never have come to Zurich if he had known what was good for him. Clearly, Calvin wanted Servetus dead, and he got what he wanted. The city magistrates condemned him to burning at the stake. Granted, Calvin suggested that they consider a more humane means of execution, but his request was dismissed. (How kind of you, John.) Nevertheless, Calvin, satisfied with his opponent's demise, wrote afterward in defense of his actions:

> Servetus . . . suffered the penalty due to his heresies, but was it by my will? Certainly, his arrogance destroyed him not less than

> his impiety...posterity owes me a debt of gratitude for having purged the Church of so pernicious a monster.

Wow. I probably just ruined your hope in humanity. It's a difficult chapter, I know. I wish these kinds of things weren't part of our history. But it is. And who do we have to thank for these delightful stories? (I hope my sarcasm is evident.) You guessed it — the religious spirit. When we read these accounts, it's important to remember that everyone who persecuted others for their beliefs was thoroughly convinced that they were correct. They were persuaded that their actions were blessed and affirmed by God. This is why we must be careful when we are "sure" that we are right. Whether Catholic or Protestant, Calvinist or Armenian, or any other sect or group, no one is immune to the influence of the religious spirit. If there's one thing our brief history lesson has made apparent, it's that the religious spirit doesn't play fair or pick sides. Let me say that again. The spirit of religion does not pick sides.

The goal of the enemy is not to win. He has already lost. His ultimate goal (if I could use a sports analogy here) is to keep the Church from scoring. And if he can get the Church to turn on itself, he has made his job much more manageable.

ZEALOUS MISDIRECTION

Have you ever embarrassed yourself in front of a group of people? I have plenty of times. But one, in particular, comes to memory. I'm on the kickball field at my elementary school. I'm in third grade. It's December, but it's Alabama, so we can still play kickball outside without freezing. So I'm up to the plate to kick, wearing a hunter-green sweatshirt with a handmade appliqué Santa Claus on the front. The pitcher launches the ball right at me. As it flies, skimming the ground just above the sandy recess yard, I ready my feet for the kick of a lifetime.

I can see it now, my foot making contact just below center, the rubber reverberating with the powerful drive of my velcro sneakers; the ball soaring over the heads of the basemen, across the road, and landing safely into the ditch. I am suddenly rushed by my teammates, lifted into the air, and praised with chants of my greatness. And all of this is in slow motion for dramatic effect.

Except, that's not exactly how it happened. Here's how it went down. As the kickball hurled toward me, I hesitated, not being a great judge of distance. As I ran forward to move in for the kick, I moved too quickly. The next thing I knew, the kickball hit my legs, and I flew into the air backward in slow motion. My back slammed the dirt first, then my legs and head.

It was a total Charlie Brown and Lucy moment when she snatches the football right before he kicks. Not only did all the boys on the field erupt in uncontrollable laughter, but so did our P.E. teacher, Coach Rayburn. Worse than that, the girls playing their game across the recess yard laughed at me too! In one instant, I was the laughingstock of the entire 3rd grade at Elba Elementary School.

How would I ever recover from the embarrassment? Well, I did. Well, mostly. My future wife, who was also in the recess yard that day, remembers that moment. She says now that she felt sorry for the kid in the Santa sweatshirt hitting the dirt. And she swears she didn't laugh.

My kickball failure is nothing compared to the instant regret defensive lineman Jim Marshall of the Minnesota Vikings must have felt during a game against the San Francisco 49ers in October of 1964. During a play when the 49ers fumbled a ball, Marshall snagged it and ran like a madman to the end zone. Curiously, no one followed him.

I'm sure he crossed the goal line and tossed the ball in the air, expecting uproarious cheers. But everyone in the stadium that day knew something Marshall didn't. He hadn't scored a touchdown at all.

He would say after the game, "My first inkling that something was wrong was when a 49ers player gave me a hug in the end zone." Yep. You guessed it. When Jim Marshall grabbed that loose ball, he got confused and went the wrong way! Instead of earning his team three points, the referees awarded the opposing team two points for a safety. Whew.

I'm embarrassed for him all these years later. Luckily for Jim Marshall, the Vikings pulled out a win anyway, and he went on to have a very successful career in the NFL.

Just as Jim Marshall ran the ball the wrong way into the end zone, clueless that he was scoring for the other team, the religious spirit will have us scoring points for the wrong team without even realizing we're doing it. Again, this dragon is not in it to win it. He just wants us to lose. The religious spirit will convince us that we are doing God a favor in "defending the faith" or "proclaiming the truth." But in reality, we bring harm and division among our team, the Body of Christ.

At the beginning of this book, I said, "It is possible to be right and wrong at the same time." Just because our facts are correct doesn't mean we are valid in the way we communicate those facts. It matters not only what we say but how and even when we say it. Likewise, we can act, motivated by a zeal for what is right, while tearing down more than we build up.

A.W. Tozer once said, "The truth is that though all godly persons are zealous, not all zealous people are godly." We can have the best intentions but produce the worst results. That's why we must always be motivated by love. We must stay aware of the spirit in which we're operating. This takes daily, even moment-by-moment, submission to the Holy Spirit, the Great Examiner of hearts. So, the next time your zeal has you running the ball down the field, maybe look up and check which direction you are running.

CHAPTER ELEVEN
Dragon Speech

When my wife and I were newlyweds, we had the opportunity to tour the National Holocaust Museum in Washington, D.C. As we wandered those halls for hours, I began to piece together how a government could systematically murder millions in death camps while many of its citizens stood idly by. The Nazi Germany we read about in history didn't just happen overnight. The tragedy of the Final Solution was not a quick and hasty decision.

Instead, it was the culmination of a years-long process. A carefully constructed propaganda machine had poisoned the minds and hearts of the people of Germany in the 1930s and 40s, not only stirring up the nationalist spirit and a renewed vision of the fatherland but, more insidiously, the belief that they were the "master race." In their minds, the Jews of Europe were a disease to be eradicated. The Ministry of Propaganda, led by Josef Goebbels, was created to shape the Nazi nation's ideas and ideals. They achieved this by changing how people thought by changing the meaning of language.

Certain words and phrases were hijacked for sinister purposes. The Jewish people were referred to as "rats" or other animals. Even the depictions of Jews in their propaganda appeared animal-like or sub-human. So, when the time came to enact the removal and eventual extermination of the Jews from Europe, the antisemitic pump was primed, and the unspeakable was seen, for many at the time, as justified.

George Orwell said, "If thought corrupts language, language can also corrupt thought."

Language is powerful. Language creates culture. The world in which we live has been shaped positively by the writings of thinkers who challenged the status quo of their day and envisioned a brighter future. So, it would be ludicrous to say that language itself is evil just because it has been misused. It is simply a medium through which change comes when ideas are shared.

Still, history teaches us that words can bring about long-lasting negative impacts and even suffering. And just because the Bible is authoritatively true doesn't mean it is immune to misuse. Here in the United States, in the Antebellum South, slavery was seen by many as an acceptable means of economic prosperity. In this modern era, it can become easy for us to remove ourselves from the awful realities of slavery in our nation's past. Yet, reminders surround us in my city of Savannah, Georgia.

Finger-shaped indentations in the gray brick fashioned by the hands of enslaved people are still visible in some structures downtown. Two miles west of downtown Savannah, near Otis Brock Elementary School, is a parcel of land known as the site of The Weeping Time. The old Ten Broeck Race Track used to occupy the landscape and was the backdrop for one of the largest slave auctions in U.S. history. In early March 1859, over 400 African American enslaved men, women, and children were sold to alleviate the mounting debt of a nearby plantation owner named Pierce Mease Butler.

A torrential downpour plagued the two-day sale. Some families were sold together as a unit. Others were separated, never to reunite. Children old enough to work were separated from their parents and siblings. Young couples not yet married were torn apart, never seeing each other again. Everyone lost something that day. Some watched their family members loaded onto wagons and train cars, waving goodbye for the last time.

They lost their dignity as men bought and sold their fellow men underneath the weeping sky. The stories still haunt us, and that traumatic event sometimes seems to hang like a shadow over the community. But this story, while a more dramatic and notable event, was one of many like it. Slavery was a part of life in the South. Human beings were bought and sold all the time. So the horror was ongoing, not isolated to one event.

Where was the Church when all of this was happening? Where were the voices willing to call out the injustices they witnessed right before their eyes? It would seem that the most likely people who would speak up against slavery were people of faith, right? Not at all. A few exceptions, like William Wilberforce, spoke up and brought lasting reform. But for the most part, the Church of the South accepted slavery. Their position was justified as easily as a few page-turns in the family Bible. Passages like this one from Paul's letter to the Ephesians were the enslavers' proof text that God approved of the practice:

> Slaves, obey your earthly masters with respect and fear, and with sincerity of heart, just as you would obey Christ. Obey them not only to win their favor when their eye is on you, but as slaves of Christ, doing the will of God from your heart. Serve whole-heartedly, as if you were serving the Lord, not people, because you know that the Lord will reward each one for whatever good they do, whether they are slave or free.
>
> EPHESIANS 6:5-8 NIV

It has been argued (a point on which I agree) that Paul is not condoning slavery here but rather speaking to enslaved people who now follow Christ. He points out that even in the cultural context where slavery was considered "normal," there is another way to live. The way of Jesus can be lived out regardless of the situation. But the more shocking statement from Paul is in the following verse:

> And masters, treat your slaves in the same way. Do not threaten them, since you know that He who is both their Master and yours is in heaven, and there is no favoritism with Him.

EPHESIANS 6:9 NIV

Far from condoning slavery, Paul is leveling the playing field and proclaiming that the lines separating slave and master are nothing in the Kingdom. This new way of life supersedes our cultural constructs and calls for radical love and the dignity of all people. Yet, this passage and others like it were used to justify the cruel practice of slavery. This is not the only instance in which the Bible or religious language has been used to justify, control, or even humiliate people. Unfortunately, it seems to be a favorite tactic of the enemy.

SINISTER SEMANTICS

I remember the morning of September 11, 2001, like yesterday. I was a college student. Getting ready for class that morning, I saw something briefly on the news about a plane crash but headed out the door, not realizing the gravity of the situation.

By the time I got to my English class, the whole campus was buzzing with the news that not one, but two commercial airliners had crashed into the Twin Towers of the World Trade Center in New York City. Soon after, we heard another plane had flown into the Pentagon, and yet another went down in Shanksville, PA, missing its intended target, thanks to the heroic efforts of a brave group of passengers. The 19 hijackers who executed the well-organized terrorist attack on U.S. soil were responsible for the deaths of over 2,900 people.

A hijacker illegally takes control of an aircraft or other vehicle, forcing it to go a different route. The religious spirit loves to hijack language for its own purposes. Words meant to express meaning in one sense are seized and perverted for sinister purposes. Let's take the word "grace," for example. Many have twisted this term to justify their sin by saying, "We're under grace. It's ok! That means Jesus is cool with it."

This is a far cry from the "grace" that the Apostle Paul encouraged the believers in Rome to embrace: "What shall we say then? Are we to continue in sin that grace may abound? By no means! How can we who died to sin still live in it?" (Romans 6:1-2 ESV). Paul warns against such an attitude toward the grace of God and tells us to be careful not to take advantage of such a gift. While it is true that the grace we have received from God is a free gift, if we have genuinely received grace, why in the world would we want to abuse it?

Scripture contains additional instances where the true essence of words has been distorted or misrepresented. Concepts like love and truth have been mislabeled by many. We have called love what it is not, and we have diluted truth to the point that it no longer means anything, and yet we don't change the words themselves. It's still "love" and "truth." In some Christian circles, the gift of prophecy has been weaponized to manipulate and control others. In other circles, the idea of holiness has taken on a strictly outward display of piety, ignoring the heart almost entirely.

I love the concept of "honor." Teachings I've heard on the subject have entirely changed how I relate to people. I learned early on that honoring someone meant recognizing and affirming the value of a person. As a pastor, I've taught about honor in this light. But I've received helpful feedback from some of my brothers and sisters in Christ who have had a very different experience and history with that word, honor.

To them, honor was used to garner praise from those in spiritual leadership. In these environments, honor was demanded. They were shamed if they didn't "honor" the "man of God" enough. Since this had never been my experience, I didn't realize that some people in our church were interpreting something utterly different than what I meant when I mentioned the subject of honor.

Over the past few years, especially, the political climate in America has been a war of words. Politicians routinely hurl accusations at each other to win, but it has worsened in the last decade. With the explosion of social media, everyone now has a megaphone. The problem is the voices are just echoing each other to the degree that vast swathes of the culture are swept into a frenzy of group thought almost overnight.

Cultural buzzwords surrounding "Christian Nationalism" and "Critical Race Theory," for example, have been hurled at opposing views to demonize the other side. Because, after all, in the minds of many, the end goal is to win the argument and not engage in conversation that leads to understanding. News outlets have done little to help the situation. These days, a person can tune in to whatever news source gives credence to whatever they believe. As a result, we have created echo chambers that have further divided us.

Contrary to popular belief among Christians, God doesn't subscribe to one news feed over the other. His truth surpasses it all. Words are beautiful, helpful, and necessary. But when words become weapons, they can be deadly. The adage, "Sticks and stones may break my bones, but words can never hurt me," is untrue. Can you see by now that there is a spirit behind all of this? Dragon speech is what it is. Unfortunately, the religious spirit has twisted so much of our terminology in the Church that we often must go into great detail to describe what we mean when we use such terms. How we use our words is so important.

The religious spirit brings division wherever it's allowed. It thrives in isolation. Whenever we isolate ourselves from the rest of the Body of Christ, we put ourselves in the enemy's crosshairs. Isolation is a slippery slope.

Isolation breeds suspicion.

Suspicion breeds gossip.

Gossip breeds division.

Division breeds death.

Add in a measure of pain, and this is the recipe for cynicism and criticism in the body of Christ. Hurt people hurt people. Pain and unhealed trauma leave us looking through a lens that doesn't represent the truth. When it happens in the Church, division is the byproduct. But behind all of it is the religious spirit working in the background to bring more division and pain.

Isolation isn't just personal. Isolation can be corporate. It comes in the form of group thinking. Remember those echo chambers? They're the product of what we construct around ourselves. Depending on what "camp" of Christianity you're in, chances are you've heard some pretty damning charges against other Christians outside the camp. Words like "cult" and "heretics" have wrongly been used to label those with whom we disagree on secondary issues.

This greatly grieves the heart of the Father, and it has to stop. Sure, we've all got our ideas on what the Church should look like and how it should function. We all have our version of correct theology and sound doctrine. But we are called to love the Church, not our version of it, not our glorified idea of what it should be, but the Church, as it is, in its brokenness, because that is what Jesus does. The moment we label a segment of the Body of Christ as anything but the "true" Church, we have exempted them from our love. If we're not careful, we can actually cause damage to the Church by trying to "fix" it. This is really tempting to do when we love our idea of community rather than the community itself.

As a fellow member of the Body of Christ, I ask you to resist the urge to rescue the Church from itself. Instead, just love it, pray for it, and let Jesus do what only He can do. Let us all heed the words of our Savior when He said:

> Why do you look at the speck of sawdust in your brother's eye and pay no attention to the plank in your own eye? How can you say to your brother, "Let me take the speck out of your eye," when all the time there is a plank in your own eye? You hypocrite, first take the plank out of your own eye, and then you will see clearly to remove the speck from your brother's eye.
>
> MATTHEW 7:3-5 NIV

So, how do we eradicate the religious spirit from the Church? It all starts with a look in the mirror. Are you ready?

CHAPTER THIRTEEN
Confronting the Dragon

As a kid, I spent a lot of time at my Granny and Paw Akridge's house. My Paw went to Heaven when I was six years old, so I have few memories of him, but they are happy ones. He often took me on walks down the dirt road near their house. It was always an adventure.

I remember him stooping down to teach me what kind of animals had left the tracks in the soft dirt and the names of trees that grew along our path. He never tired of my endless questions! One day, as we were preparing for our adventure, he put a jacket on me and said,

"If you get too cold, we'll turn around and go home, okay?"

It was pretty chilly outside that day, so it's a wonder that Granny let him take me. As we started our journey, we neared an old house on the corner beside the dirt road. We had to walk by that house every time we went on walks. I always thought it looked spooky. But the real problem for me was what was inside the chain-link fence. A bulldog. A very vocal bulldog.

That day, just like all the others, he saw us coming and began his territorial display.

"Now, don't be scared of that dog. He's in a fence. He won't hurt you. I won't let him get you," Paw said.

My heart was pounding. I was terrified of that dog! Usually, Paw's gentle reassurance was enough for me to overcome my fear and walk on by. Not that day. I stopped and pulled Paw's hand.

"I'm getting a little bit cold," I said.

He smiled, seeing right through my excuse.

"Do you want to turn around and go back?" he asked.

"Yes," I said.

That day, I let that bark rob me of an adventure. Fear got the best of me. But my decision to turn back that day wasn't a life-altering decision. Paw and I would take that walk again numerous times. But this story teaches us a bigger lesson. Fear can cause us to miss out on the most important moments of our lives. Our fears guard the thresholds of our future. Thresholds are divine moments of invitation into our destiny. At thresholds, we are given a choice. We can listen to the barking lies of the enemy, consider his threats, let fear win, and turn back. Or we can press on, pull in close to the Father, round the corner, and go on the most incredible adventure of our lives! Just keep walking. Resist the lies and keep pressing forward, as scary or awkward as it feels...even if it feels wrong. God's truth trumps our feelings, emotional attachments, and religious traditions.

You don't slay dragons by talking about slaying dragons. It's time to get to work!

I'm obliged to give you a heads-up about what we're about to do. In short, when you rouse a dragon, you can always expect fire. Don't be surprised if the dragon gets agitated when you start poking around in its lair. If we are to eradicate the influence of the religious spirit from our lives, we need to expect the enemy to resist.

SPIRITUAL BURNS

Several years ago, my dad cooked burgers for a concession stand at our local high school football game. He opened the grill just like he had every other time, except this time, a massive ball of flames engulfed his face. When the smoke cleared, his eyebrows, lashes, and even some of the hair on his head were singed. His face was red from the heat but not badly burned. But we learned something that day about burns. A doctor told him that despite no outward signs of severe burns, he needed to get to the nearest burn center as soon as possible. What we were unaware of until that moment was that facial burns significantly increase the risk of respiratory burns. If inhaled, the fire, smoke, and heat can burn the inside of the throat, nasal passage, and even lungs. It would only be possible to know the damage once the airway became inflamed. Then, more serious complications could arise, and the inflammation could obstruct the airway. We drove a couple of hours to the burn center that night, and the good news was that there was no internal damage.

Just as the effects of inhaling smoke or flames can go unnoticed until more significant problems show up, the "smoke" and "fire" of the religious dragon can damage our hearts, but we might not be aware until we are confronted with it. I suspect that some parts of this book have been triggering to you. I know you may be experiencing some discomfort, even deep pain, over what you've experienced in a religious setting. The dragon itself may have burned you.

Church hurt is not easy to go through or get over. I am aware of the importance of recognizing the pain experienced by many of my readers before delving into this chapter, so I will proceed with sensitivity and understanding. My heart for you is that you would encounter the love of a good Father and begin the healing process with Him or take one more step toward wholeness.

My heart has been grieved lately as stories of moral failure, abuse, financial improprieties, and other issues have been exposed in the global Church. Many of these situations involved respected and beloved leaders. Spiritual abuse that has run rampant in the shadows is coming to light. I'm well aware that some have used the term "spiritual abuse" flippantly in reaction to something challenging in their church community, but not necessarily damaging. But for every person's story like this, dozens of others have endured horrifying experiences with the Church. Not only has spiritual abuse plagued the institution, but physical, emotional, and sexual abuse have also been all too common. I've heard stories of people who, as children, were molested in the Church, a place that was supposed to be safe, by people who were supposed to be trustworthy and loving.

I've witnessed some of the most vile hatred spewed in the name of God. I am a pastor who loves the Church as a whole, but honestly, I don't blame anyone for deconstructing their faith in light of these horrors and inconsistencies. It's been hard to watch the story unfold before our eyes. It's been even harder for the survivors of religious abuse. But it was never meant to be this way. Manipulation, fear, secrecy, and control are not fruits of the Holy Spirit, yet they have been the fruit of many a ministry and are even considered normal.

If a pastor or other spiritual leader has hurt you, intentionally or unintentionally, I can understand your pain. I acknowledge that spiritual abuse is real and has harmed many. As a spiritual leader in the Church, I want to say that I am so sorry that someone in my position hurt you, tainted your view of your Heavenly Father, or damaged your ability to trust.

I can say from experience that much of what I've established in this book as the religious spirit is perpetuated by leaders in the Church simply because they learned it from others. In many faith circles, coercion and control are seen as par for the course in ministry. Please realize that this way of thinking stems from many leaders being hurt and influenced by the dragon themselves. This is not meant to excuse the pain that may have been caused. It's just the way it is. But it doesn't have to be for you any longer. There is a way forward.

I encourage you to forgive. Be healed. Let the love of God meet you in your pain. As hard as it may be, I encourage you to embrace the Church; don't run from it. Find wholeness in the community of the broken and burned out. The most beautiful expressions of faith in Jesus are found in the ashes of past ruin.

If you're ready, take a moment and pray. Talk to God openly and honestly about your pain. Tell Him what's on your heart, and invite the Healer to bind up your broken heart, restore your soul, and help you regain trust. If you don't know where to start, I'll include a little prayer you can put in your own words:

> *Father, you know my heart. You know that people have hurt me that I once trusted, people I admired, who were supposed to be my role models in the faith. I have carried a wound that I've not known how to manage and cannot heal on my own. I'm ready now. Holy Spirit, I ask You to give me the grace to forgive those who've hurt me. I choose forgiveness today. I may not feel it right now, but I choose to obey, knowing the feelings will come later. Jesus, I need You to reveal who You really are to me. My ideas about you have been influenced by others who did not represent You well. Help me rediscover You, starting today. Heal my heart. Renew my mind. I ask this in Your name, Jesus. Amen.*

Good job. Keep moving forward with Jesus. Don't give up on the Church. As you heal and keep choosing forgiveness and walking in deep friendship with God, you will become the change you long to see in the Church.

LET'S HAVE A FUNERAL

We've been learning to identify the spirit of religion, but now we're moving into resistance mode. How do we resist this dragon? Well, since the essence of religion concerns mindsets, defeating the dragon means replacing old destructive attitudes with new ones. Remember, this fight is not about identifying and resisting everyone else's dragons but rather about what we will do about our own lives.

Do we see it in others? If we're discerning, yes. But this is not about picking fights. Think of how Jesus confronted the religious spirit. He called it out, for sure, but He also stayed silent in the face of accusation.

His motivation was not self-preservation or self-defense. His motivation was love for the people the religious spirit had oppressed.

So, the first step to dragon slaying is taking our splinter-picking glasses off and dealing with our own hearts. Then, we can gently and compassionately lead others into freedom as well. That is my hope for you. I want you to experience the freedom I've experienced and continue to experience as I grow.

What if the initial step to kill the dragon is to kill some things in us first? What if the prerequisite for slaying dragons is death to self? After all, the first call of the gospel is to take up our cross, just as Jesus did. Death to self is the precursor to personal revival. Again, this is about mindset.

In 2012, while serving as a worship leader and youth pastor at a rural church in Alabama, I had a defining encounter with God that has marked my life. I refer to it as "my funeral" because this encounter gave me a profound awareness of what it means to be crucified with Christ.

It all started after a Sunday morning service. As I closed the piano after the service ended, my heart was so grieved, not because of anything that happened in morning worship but because of what was happening in me. Afterward, as I sat at our kitchen table, the heaviness was so intense that I told my wife I wasn't hungry and needed to walk back to the church building to pray.

I kept hearing the word "mourn" in my mind, but I didn't know why I was sensing that word, other than it felt like I was doing just that — mourning. So, I got up from the table, walked across the street, and unlocked the doors to the auditorium. I turned the lock and made my way up the aisle. The heaviness in my soul became more intense as I went up the stairs to the platform and collapsed into tears. The only way to describe it was that in this season of my life, I felt grossly inadequate for what God was calling me to do. The call to come up the mountain with Him and know Him more than ever was heavy on my heart, but at the same time, I felt so unworthy.

That afternoon was a tipping point in my life. No longer could I play games or live in defeat. I told God, "If this is all there is to the Christian life, then I want to die. I don't want to go on living if there is no victory in it." I wasn't suicidal. I was just at the end of my rope spiritually. Another way to put it is that I was "poor in spirit" (Matthew 5:3). Little did I know, Jesus was about to reveal Himself to me in a way I had never experienced before. My poverty-stricken soul was about to receive an inheritance beyond my comprehension.

As I lay on that carpet and wept until it was soaked with my tears, mourning my sin and miserable condition, I cried repeatedly, "I want to be dead. I want to be dead!" I meant that in a spiritual sense. I wanted to be completely dead to sin and alive in God. But an honesty poured from my heart that if living dead to sin wasn't possible, life wasn't worth living. It was a sad, messy moment that I'm glad no one else saw.

But it was also beautiful because, in the middle of my wailing and weeping, Jesus spoke. I didn't hear Him with my ears, but His still, small voice within me felt like a shout that permeated my whole being. "You already are," He said. "You just don't know it." It stopped me in my tracks.

I expected Him to answer my cry to die once and for all. I was expecting death or something else. But the "something else" was His reminding me of something I knew but had never fully known experientially. I was already dead. Suddenly, the words from Galatians 2:20 traveled like a shockwave through my soul, tearing down years of religious lies and misplaced hope: "I have been crucified with Christ; it is no longer I who live, but Christ lives in me; and the life which I now live in the flesh I live by faith in the Son of God, who loved me and gave Himself for me."

What happened next is hard to explain, and I never feel I do it justice whenever I tell my story. Encounters with God don't fit in boxes that make total sense. As this seemingly new revelation that I was, in fact, "crucified with Christ" took hold of me, I saw a mental picture of the wounds of Jesus. The crucifixion played out like a movie before me, except it all happened in a second or two. I saw the crown of thorns on Jesus's head, the nails in His hands and feet, the torn flesh on His back from the whipping, and the spear being thrust into His side. And at the same time, I saw that those wounds were my own. I could almost feel them in my own body.

In a matter of seconds, my whole world changed. To say the "lightbulb switched on" would be an understatement. The gospel took on an entirely new application for me. Not only was Jesus crucified for me, but I was crucified with Him. I was a new creation, not of my own earning or effort. My victory wasn't dependent upon my track record. I was a brand new person because I died with Jesus. And now my life is in Him. My life is His.

My life that I live in this flesh and blood reality is by faith in the Son of God.

Until that moment, my faith was in my performance. I had always believed that God was happy with me if I was doing well in life. But when I wasn't living up to the standard I had in my mind, I thought God hated me. I would never articulate it in those words, but that's exactly how I had lived up to that point. It took my being entirely bankrupt to see that I had more in Christ than I could have ever hoped.

I finally began to understand what "Christ in me, the hope of glory" was all about (Colossians 1:27). The religious spirit had robbed me of what I already had! The dragon was claiming an inheritance that belonged to me! When I realized that the old me was truly dead, that I was alive in Christ, and that everything that belongs to Him was mine, it changed everything. But the dragon didn't receive its mortal wound that day on the carpet of my old church. No. The dragon was defeated at the cross!

> And you, who were dead in your trespasses and the uncircumcision of your flesh, God made alive together with Him, having forgiven us all our trespasses, by canceling the record of debt that stood against us with its legal demands. This He set aside, nailing it to the cross. He disarmed the rulers and authorities and put them to open shame, by triumphing over them in Him.
>
> COLOSSIANS 2:13-15 ESV

Let that sink in. The enemy who seeks to blind us and bind us with lies was defeated and disarmed at Calvary. He has no authority to sit on a treasure that doesn't belong to him. He has no right to keep us in the dark about what we possess in Jesus. The greatest weapon against the religious spirit is the knowledge of the true gospel, not a powerless gospel that waits on us to live up to its efficacy, but rather a beautiful gospel that saves us and sustains us by grace alone! There is so much power in that! "For I am not ashamed of the gospel, because it is the power of God that brings salvation to everyone who believes" (Romans 1:16 NIV). The religious spirit says: it's about what you do. The gospel shouts: it's about what He did.

The sooner we let the gospel penetrate our hearts and believe it, the sooner that old dragon will be on the run. Even though we are technically dead to sin and alive to God, we must apply that truth to our lives. We can say we're living in victory but live in defeat. We can say we're dead to sin but not live it out. We must walk what we talk. We must stay vigilant to avoid slipping back into old mindsets.

HITLIST

Recently, the Lord challenged me to do a deep dive into the following areas of my life, and I have challenged our church to do the same. I've come to believe that four things tremendously influence whether or not we will steward our freedom well. These four are, without a doubt, primary targets of the religious spirit. We must die in these four areas to eliminate religion's influence.

Let's start with control. Control and manipulation are dragon tactics. It's witchcraft, to be honest, and that has no place in the life of a Christ follower. The truth is, our attempts at control are futile and do nothing but frustrate us and lead to burnout.

We try to control our circumstances, only to find out we have no control over our circumstances. In fact, the best way to lose control is to try to control everything. That doesn't mean we should lower our expectations for the best, but we cannot marry our expectations. We will get disappointed when we put our hope in anything but God. Friend, hear me out. Outcomes are not yours to control. Give it to God.

We not only try to control our circumstances, but we often try to control people, too. I will say something you may have heard before, but I need you to really get this one. It will help you so much: It's not your job to change anybody.

Really, it's not. I know religion has taught you that it is, but it's not your job to change others. When we attempt to control our spouse, it certainly doesn't produce a happy marriage. All it does is make one spouse walk on eggshells and the other never satisfied. When we try to control our kids, whether saving them from their own choices or restricting choices to the point that they don't have any say in their own lives, it makes for kids who become adults who haven't learned how to manage themselves. We do all this in the name of love, of course. But isn't it really more fear than love? Here's the deal. You can control your children, or you can have a connection with them. You can't have both. This goes for all of our relationships, not just marriage and family.

Did you know that we can attempt to control God? No one would admit that because it sounds preposterous. No one can control God, right? But we think we can. Here's what I mean. Every move of God throughout history has come with a temptation to control. Revival, for example, can be messy. It's rarely neat and tidy. There have always been people who do crazy things out of their own flesh. But just because it may seem weird to us doesn't mean it's not God.

When we face something we don't understand, we tend to try to fit it into something we can understand...or control. That's why we must continually renew our commitment to "presence over preference." Control will shut down a move of God, and the religious spirit will call it wisdom and order. Control — whether controlling circumstances, people, or God Himself — is rooted in fear. If we're honest, we manipulate others because we fear what they might do.

We try to manage outcomes because we fear how things will turn out. We want to maintain control of the reins when God moves because it feels unsafe. John, "the beloved," gives us insight into the root of control and how to overcome it: "There is no fear in love. But perfect love drives out fear, because fear has to do with punishment. The one who fears is not made perfect in love." (1 John 4:18 NIV)

If love is what casts out fear, then the cure for controlling people is loving them. And if fear results from placing our faith in the wrong thing, then the cure for control is simply trusting God. How many of our stressors would melt away if we simply chose to trust Him? Are your kids making terrible decisions? Instead of controlling them, guide them, yes, but trust God with your kids.

If your circumstances seem dire, try trusting God with whatever is stressing you out instead of worrying and trying to change them. If letting go of the reins seems terrifying to you as a leader, try trusting Him with your organization's or church's direction for a change. If nothing else, life is way more enjoyable that way! It may not be predictable, but it will be more fruitful and fulfilling. I've been on both sides and prefer letting God do His thing. He's way better at it than I am!

Next, we're confronting offense. I've given it some attention in previous chapters but want to lean in more here. Offense is not just about hurt feelings. Offense is part of a much larger issue because offense is not an isolated emotional or relational event. Offense is part of a cycle, a downward spiral into destruction. And I'm not being overly dramatic with that statement. Let me illustrate it. The cycle looks like this:

Unchecked Pride

The catalyst for the downward spiral is unchecked pride. At its heart, pride convinces us that we deserve something; furthermore, we deserve something we are not getting from other people, or maybe even from God.

Entitlement

This is an inward expression of our pride that makes us more important in our own eyes than we ought to be. Entitlement sets the stage for offense to land. Put another way, entitlement is the soil in which offense takes root.

Offense

This stems from a situational event that is hurtful or offensive. It is not uncommon to encounter offense. For example, we might get offended by a comment made by someone who wasn't thinking when they spoke. Or we might experience offense because someone intentionally hurt us. But offense is just an event unless we give it space to grow. When we don't deal with our offenses, they can grow into something we didn't want or see coming.

Resentment

If offense is situational, then resentment is personal. At this point, it's no longer only about what happened. It's about the person who did it. This is where love erodes, and we begin to see others as the enemy. And when we see people as the problem, we will inevitably attack people.

Bitterness

If offense is situational and resentment is personal, bitterness is pervasive. By the time we reach this level, it's no longer about the offense or the person who offended us. Now, we are offendable because we have become bitter. Our filter has been compromised, and we now see life through a pain lens. Unforgiveness has dug its roots deep into our hearts. This is a dangerous place to be. The writer of Hebrews illustrates just how destructive it is:

> Strive for peace with everyone, and for the holiness without which no one will see the Lord. See to it that no one fails to obtain the grace of God; that no root of bitterness springs up and causes trouble, and by it many become defiled.
>
> HEBREWS 12:14-15 ESV

Notice in these verses that bitterness doesn't just affect us and how we see the world. The bitterness growing within us doesn't stay put. Instead, it branches out and spreads to others.

Defiling Influence

This outward expression of bitterness causes others to follow you down the path of destruction. How scary is it that our influence in someone's life could be the factor that ruins their life? That's exactly what happens when we allow bitterness to live unchecked. It spreads to others.

Slander and Accusation

Jesus said, "Out of the abundance of the heart, the mouth speaks" (Luke 6:45). A bitter heart speaks slander. When we talk with others about people who offended us, we start the process of offense, resentment, and bitterness in someone else. That's why the most important action we can take with offense is to have a conversation with the person or people who offended us, not everyone else. It is so tempting to run and tell our friends when we are hurt because we need their input or sympathy. But resist the urge. You could be inviting offense into the ones you love the most.

> If your brother sins against you, go and tell him his fault, between you and him alone. If he listens to you, you have gained your brother. But if he does not listen, take one or two others along with you, that every charge may be established by the evidence of two or three witnesses.
>
> MATTHEW 18:15-16 ESV

When we don't deal with offense immediately and instead allow the bitter root to have its way with us, we can become so bitter that we go from avoiding offense, to expecting to be offended, to seeking offense! I call this type of person an "offense magnet." They've become so jaded that they can no longer see the good in people, only the bad. And they are offended by everything. What a miserable life! But Jesus is the Healer. No one is too far to experience healing and freedom from rejection and the pain of the past. So if you find yourself in that place, take a moment and ask Jesus to heal you of your wounds. Choose to forgive, have the conversation, and make a counseling appointment. Do whatever you have to do to begin your journey toward healing.

CRITICISM

Criticism toward others, especially in the Church, can be so hurtful. It is often a form of control, as we have already discussed. It's been around awhile. Paul had to address a critical spirit in the Church at Ephesus in his letter to them: "Let no corrupting talk come out of your mouths, but only such as is good for building up, as fits the occasion, that it may give grace to those who hear." (Ephesians 4:29 ESV)

This verse is often quoted to discourage cursing, and while I don't think we should be potty-mouths, I don't believe this is what Paul was addressing here. The "corrupting talk" he's discouraging them from engaging in is contrasted by his phrase, "but only such as is good for building up." The opposite of building up is tearing down. He warned the believers not to tear each other down with their words but to instead build each other up with their speech.

I've seen people tear down others in the Church just because of disagreements or preferences. Criticism and accusation are from the same womb. And when we criticize, we can sound a lot like the Accuser, Satan himself. I sure don't want to partner with the Accuser. Criticism has to go! I've heard, "The most critical people are often most critical of themselves." If that's true (and my experience pastoring people for many years tells me that it is), then maybe criticism dies when we are no longer critical of ourselves. Shame can get us down. It can make us feel worthless and unlovable and, in turn, cause us to think of others the same way we think about ourselves. A critical spirit is healed by understanding our new identity in Christ. Criticism is the language of spiritual orphans. Self-acceptance and growth into becoming like Christ is the journey of spiritual sons and daughters.

FEAR OF MAN

Lastly, the fear of man has to die. Proverbs 29:25 says, "The fear of man lays a snare, but whoever trusts in the Lord is safe." Fearing what people think is an actual trap. The bait is flattery. Don't fall for it. Accept compliments and receive honor humbly, but let flattery go in one ear and out the other.

It's been said, "If you live for men's praise, you will die by their criticism." Living for the applause of people is one of the hallmark features of the religious spirit. The opinions of people shaped the religious leaders of Jesus' day. Trust me, I've let the fear of man rule my life for far longer than I care to admit. No one likes to be criticized or misunderstood — I get it. It's one of the ways we try to preserve our reputation, and yet, when we live for others' approval, we accomplish the opposite. We actually lose our reputation by seeking to please everyone. You can't make everybody happy...unless you're ice cream.

Think of it this way: Jesus was perfect, and He still had enemies. Just because you're doing it right doesn't mean you won't be criticized. In fact, doing it right is the very thing that sometimes invites criticism. There is a better way to live than to be caught in the trap of the fear of man! When I first began to experience freedom from this, it changed everything for me. A godly confidence provided a lens through which I could make decisions free from worrying about what anyone thought. To me, this was entirely unfamiliar territory. I've still got a long way to go in this area. I still lean too much on others' opinions at times. I believe that death to the fear of man is one of the final nails in the coffin of religion. When we let a healthy fear of the Lord rule over our fear of people, we kick some serious dragon tail.

CHAPTER THIRTEEN
Expanding Horizons

When it comes to breaking out of the religious mindset, one of the best things we can do is to expand our horizons. Small-minded thinking can paralyze us because we may never even realize there is more unless we are exposed to a world larger than our corner of it. Curiosity has always pushed the limits of human understanding. It breaks barriers. Think of the first explorers who set out to sail across the seas. They had no idea what was out there. That's why they went, for the thrill of adventure and the itch of curiosity, the quest for a better quality of life, and greater opportunities.

Have you ever heard of Robert Goddard? In his later years, he would develop the world's first liquid-fueled rocket — the precursor to later rocket engineering that would ultimately take the first humans to the moon. As a young boy who had just read H.G. Wells' First Men In The Moon, Goddard climbed a tree and looked up into the sky. He later wrote:

> As I looked toward the fields at the east, I imagined how wonderful it would be to make some device which had even the possibility of ascending to Mars. Such a device would soar up, up, beyond the atmosphere, toward the stars. I was a different boy when I descended the tree from when I ascended.

I love that story. The curiosity of one boy ultimately got us to the moon. And an interesting side note is that Buzz Aldrin would carry a copy of Goddard's biography on Apollo 11, the first lunar mission to land on the moon.

Exploration requires us to leave the comforts of the familiar. Adventure is not safe. That's what makes it an adventure. When curiosity and hunger surpass fear, that's when courage kicks in. Nearly every pioneer in every field has been criticized and ridiculed. Those on the front lines of something new aren't swayed by those who hurl cheap shots from cushioned seats.

For some reason, the Church seems to be an institution that discourages change and even resorts to fear tactics to keep people in line or ensure nothing breaks the status quo. Unfortunately, the status quo is en vogue in the Church. It could be that the very spirit of religion we've been discussing is behind the stifling of creative advancements. If I were the enemy, I would utilize all my resources to ensure the Church doesn't get adventurous! I believe an innovative, courageous, and committed Church is one of the most dangerous entities on the planet!

PUSHING THE LIMITS

While writing this book, I have pushed through many moments of writer's block. I'm sure you've felt stuck before, too. However, I've found that something as simple as a walk can bring a fresh perspective and allow me to return to the writing desk with a clear head.

When it comes to being stuck spiritually, the solution is the same. Sometimes we can get into a rut and become accustomed to only seeing the world through a familiar lens. Getting comfortable and complacent is easy. Sometimes we need to change our routine or go on a retreat to reset our souls. Likewise, when we become comfortable and familiar with our particular "brand" of Christianity, we can think that is all there is. As a result, our idea of a life in God is truncated, even myopic. And worse, when we become so stuck in our ways and committed to certain convictions that we are no longer open to question why we do what we do or believe what we believe, we are ripe for deception. A mind made up is a breeding ground for the religious spirit.

Half-truths thrive in territory already settled. To find the broader truth, we need to explore. We need to expand our spiritual horizons to see the bigger picture. So, how does one broaden their spiritual horizons? Some fundamental shifts can help us break out of our Christian bubble and take the lid off our experience.

READ THE BIBLE

I know that sounds obvious, but I'm serious. Read the Bible with fresh eyes. The gospels are a great place to start. There's nothing wrong with devotionals or topical reading plans, but there is nothing like reading large chunks of scripture and ingesting it in full context. But our goal is not just to read the Bible. It's to encounter the Word. A good exercise is to pick a passage to read through, taking a surface-level approach. Notice the obvious things you see in the passage. Don't dig too deep at first, lest you miss the forest for the trees. Sometimes the most obvious things are the most impactful.

Once you've read it and taken notes on the surface, engage with it a little more. Reread it, but this time start asking questions about the text. Everything in the Bible is there for a reason, so don't miss the reason. Asking questions and searching out the answers is the best thing you can do to grow and get outside the box.

READ BOOKS

I'm not talking about just any books. Intentionally pick books written by people who don't see the world as you do. Read authors with whom you disagree. An open mind in an open book is a potentially life-changing experience. Don't be afraid to explore a little. Learning to "eat the meat and spit out the bones" is an excellent way to grow.

I once heard of a pastor who, upon learning of an author's view on a secondary theological stance, threw out all the books by this particular author. When we react this way to distance ourselves from whatever we see as wrong, we also cut ourselves off from the good found there.

MAKE NEW FRIENDS

One of the significant turning points in my relationship with God happened when I became friends with a few people with different views on the activity of the Holy Spirit than me. I discovered these guys weren't weird and certainly weren't "heretics." I found common ground quickly. Over time, some of my views that had no biblical merit began to change, partly due to my new friends' influence on my life. And that's not the only time that has happened to me.

I'm thankful for the variety of people God has brought into my life. I'm grateful for the different streams in the Body of Christ that flow together to form one life-giving river. Building relationships in other schools of thought and practice is like drinking from different wells. Just because you're learning from others doesn't mean you stop everything you're doing and become just like them. But it does mean that you can ask questions you didn't know needed asking and perhaps pick up some excellent habits from people you once thought were only worthy of avoidance. I'm well aware of the baggage of ecumenism – a big word that means the pursuit of unity among different denominations or churches. We can be so committed to our idea of "unity" that we no longer hold any convictions. The ecumenism I promote moves toward unity, yes, but retains the secondary convictions loosely to learn from one another. This is healthy. And, in my opinion, it is how we are meant to relate to one another in the Church.

Early in my exploration of previously unknown territory I thought, "Oh no. What if I become one of those crazy people? I don't want to go off the deep end!" I had seen plenty of people run off the tracks in their spiritual life, falling into the ditch of religious deadness on one side and religious excess on the other. At that moment, I was struck with a holy fear that, in my pursuit of more, I might fall into the ditch of religious excess and get carried away with all this "Holy Spirit stuff." A thought entered my mind. I don't know if it was an original thought, wise advice from a friend, or the gentle nudge of the Spirit. Still, my panic was put to rest by the realization that God is a good Father and He knows how to lead His kids, and if I was His kid, then I had no reason to doubt that He would lead me. So, I uttered a prayer to God that day that I've prayed many times since. "God, I want all You have for me. Nothing more, nothing less. I trust You to lead and keep me out of the ditches." And by God's grace, I think I'm still on the road.

» Have you been approaching Scripture through the lens of your own understanding? We all do to some degree. If so, stop and ask the Holy Spirit to illuminate His Word in fresh ways to you. For example, you can pray like this:

> *Holy Spirit, show me where my ideas about You and Your words have been incorrect, and open my eyes to the truth. My heart and mind are Yours to mold. Amen.*

» Does your book collection consist only of authors from a particular brand of Christianity? Branch out and read something new. Think of an author or speaker you have felt the need to distance yourself from, and buy their book or listen to one of their talks. Approach one their works with an open mind and heart. What could it hurt? Just eat the meat and spit out the bones.

» Do all your friends believe the same things? Break out of your echo chamber and make some new friends. Seriously. Reach out and invite someone who thinks differently to grab a coffee. Ask the Father to send people into your life to help shape you.

» Do you trust your heavenly Father to lead you? Are you scared of doing it wrong? Are you afraid you will mess it up? Then, stop and make a fresh surrender to Him. You can pray something like:

> *Father, I'm sorry I haven't trusted you to lead me. I believe that You are a good Shepherd. I commit my ways to you. I know you will guide my steps. Amen.*

This is spiritual warfare. It may not seem like it to you, but I assure you that action is what breaks the stronghold of the enemy. The religious spirit must be broken. You break its power over your life by changing your mind. The word repent in Greek is metanoia, which means to change one's mind or to reconsider. So, breaking religion off our lives begins with belief, but it requires more than simply knowing something. We must put feet to our beliefs, sometimes doing something physical to counteract the enemy's hold over our minds. Obedience looks like something. It requires action.

Jesus did this often when the religious leaders brought their accusations against him. I love this moment when He confronted the religious spirit by healing a man with a deformed hand:

> On another Sabbath He went into the synagogue and was teaching, and a man was there whose right hand was withered. The Pharisees and the teachers of the law were looking for a reason to accuse Jesus, so they watched Him closely to see if He would heal on the Sabbath. But Jesus knew what they were thinking and said to the man with the shriveled hand, "Get up and stand in front of everyone." So he got up and stood there. Then Jesus said to them, "I ask you, which is lawful on the Sabbath: to do good or to do evil, to save life or to destroy it?" He looked around at them all, and then said to the man, "Stretch out your hand." He did so, and his hand was completely restored.
>
> LUKE 6:6-10 NIV

Jesus didn't have to rebuke them at all. Instead, He simply asked a question and then responded with a demonstration of power that silenced the accusers.

The same principle can be applied personally. Whenever you are tempted to respond negatively to a given situation, just do the opposite of what your flesh is urging you to do. My wife learned this early on with our kids. During her years of staying home with them, she would find herself sometimes sleep-deprived and lacking the patience to handle the constant needs. If you've ever been responsible for raising small children, you know exactly how she felt. In those moments of frustration, when she wanted to lash out or respond to them in an unhealthy way, she would instead embrace them and say something kind. She found that when she acted in direct violation of her flesh, her emotions followed suit, and peace would come as she aligned her actions with the heart of the Father toward our kids.

You can apply this to nearly any situation and find that it works. For example, are you struggling to forgive someone who has hurt you? Do something kind for them without their knowing it was you. It could be as simple as attending a church that worships differently than you do. If you've never raised your hands in worship, try it. You might like it! Sometimes, in my lowest moments, the best thing I could do was act the opposite of my feelings. Now, I'm not suggesting that we discredit our emotions and ignore how we feel. Not at all. I am suggesting that we actually believe that the "joy of the Lord is our strength" and act on it.

When you worship when you don't feel like it, it isn't fake. It's faith. I remember one time when I was having a tough day. I walked into our empty house, closed the curtains, turned up some worship music, and danced my heart out. Now, I am no dancer. I was very much the wallflower at every school dance. But now and then, a good dance before the Lord turns it around for me.

While I've been writing these words, my circumstances have me feeling like I'm in the fight of my life. The last thing I wanted to do was to sit down and write more of this book. But here I am, doing exactly what the enemy doesn't want me to do. Simple obedience can be a violent act against the kingdom of darkness. The Prophet Isaiah speaks of the power of doing the right thing when you don't feel like it and the results that follow:

> Then you shall call, and the LORD will answer;
> you shall cry, and he will say, 'Here I am.'
> If you take away the yoke from your midst,
> the pointing of the finger, and speaking wickedness,

if you pour yourself out for the hungry
and satisfy the desire of the afflicted,
then shall your light rise in the darkness
and your gloom be as the noonday.
And the LORD will guide you continually
and satisfy your desire in scorched places
and make your bones strong;
and you shall be like a watered garden,
like a spring of water,
whose waters do not fail.
And your ancient ruins shall be rebuilt;
you shall raise up the foundations of many generations;
you shall be called the repairer of the breach,
the restorer of streets to dwell in.

ISAIAH 58:9-12 ESV

Notice the order there? The command came first, then the result... "then shall your light rise in the darkness and your gloom be as the noonday." Perhaps there is something right now that you can do to break the power of religion off your life. It doesn't have to be complicated, just intentional. Happy slaying.

CHAPTER FOURTEEN

A Land With No Dragons

Imagine a land with no dragons. We've seen glimpses of it sprinkled throughout history. The world has tasted God's goodness through the impact of His people over and over again. It's undeniable. The positive impact of the Church cannot be overstated. I've personally experienced the love of Christ displayed through the Christian community.

I am often blown away by the generosity and kindness I've experienced while serving and being a part of the Church. My personal experience is only a ripple in the vast ocean of charity found among God's people.

The Church's mark on the world is undeniable. Christianity has touched virtually every sphere of society. Over the centuries, the Church has founded schools, hospitals, and orphanages. Modern foster care was born in the hearts of believers who longed to see children cared for. Christians have campaigned for prison reform, adequate housing for the underprivileged, and even championed an end to the slave trade.

While many in the Church attempted to justify slavery, reformers like William Wilberforce blazed a trail of justice. He tirelessly proposed legislation to the British parliament, persistently advocating for the abolition of the slave trade and the emancipation of enslaved people. His unwavering efforts eventually led to the prohibition of the slave trade and the liberation of enslaved individuals.

The foundation for the education system, government, and law has its roots in Christian teachings, as do significant advances in women's and children's rights. The Church has gifted the world with art, literature, music, and scientific discoveries that have enriched the human race.

Granted, the history of contributions by the Church to the world is complicated. The good and the bad have often happened side by side. Despite its shortcomings, the Church has truly shaped the world as we know it for the better. I can't help but think that if the Church has accomplished so much while still being influenced by the religious spirit, what could be possible in a world where this dragon has no power?

Imagine a world where the Church is known for its unwavering commitment to living what it believes, loving Jesus wholeheartedly, and loving neighbors as they love themselves. Imagine a world in which the people of God shine so brightly in the darkness that the dramatic difference is evident to all. Imagine a Church that fights injustice, seeks to alleviate poverty, shows compassion and extends radical kindness while still standing firm on the truth of scripture.

Imagine a world in which the Church serves as a moral compass for society, a Church that truly lives out the good news it preaches. Imagine a world where the goodness of Heaven touches every corner of society, with the King's will done on earth as it is in Heaven. Imagine a Church undistracted from its mission and determined in its pursuit to demonstrate the Kingdom and make disciples of all nations. A Church with its eyes fixed on Jesus, mind set on eternity, and hands to the plow in the here and now. Imagine a powerful Church, a pure Church, a unified Church. I believe this is not just wishful thinking. I think it's possible! After all, it is the original design of the Bride of Jesus to demonstrate and prepare the way for the Kingdom of God.

REVIVAL FIRES

As a college student, I sat in a Sunday night church service listening to a visiting speaker share stories of the Great Awakenings in American History. As he recounted the moving of the Holy Spirit in our nation's history, my heart burned. And it hasn't stopped burning. The next day

I walked to the campus library and printed a copy of a book that was no longer in print that chronicled the move of God during the colonial era. Later, while sitting in my psychology class, I read the entire thing.

Hearing those stories created a hunger in me to see God do something similar in my lifetime. I yearned for revival. I wasn't exactly sure what it even was, but I knew I wanted it. Ever since then, I've studied revival history and have come to understand revival as nothing more than Jesus Himself taking His rightful place in the hearts of His people. It's easy to get distracted by everything else but the main thing. Revival brings everything back into focus. It is a return to our first love.

I now understand that revival is not limited to sporadic visitations of God among His people. Instead, revival is an invitation to the habitation of God among His people. In other words, it's not an event. It's a lifestyle. In essence, it is normal Christianity.

When I study revival history, I see a common thread woven from past to present. When society seems the most hopeless, when morality is at its lowest, when the Church is at its weakest, is when it seems God loves to burst onto the scene and display His glory. As a result, the Church wakes up to His presence and runs full sprint back to Him to fall on His grace. What usually follows is a cultural shift because the Church suddenly starts...well...being the Church again.

On an individual level, a revived heart is a heart made capable of love, a heart that can love Jesus well and, in turn, love its neighbors. When you have a community of people who experience a renewal of heart like this, things change. Those who have come to an understanding of God's beauty and love can extend that beauty and love to the world around them. Revived people are committed to reconciliation, not only with each other, but are also moved with compassion for those who don't yet know the love of Christ.

One of my favorite histories is that of the Moravians of Herrnhut, Germany. A young man named Nicolaus Zinzendorf committed to care for Christian refugees fleeing religious persecution in Europe during the 1720s. He gave a large portion of his estate to provide a place of refuge for displaced families seeking rest.

The community, comprised of people from different backgrounds and religious views, soon found it difficult to do life together. They argued over doctrinal differences such as baptism, holiness, and even end-times theology (much of what consumes the Church today). But Zinzendorf was committed to reconciliation. He urged people to make amends and to live in peace with each other. Over time, the people began to lay down their differences of opinion and turn their focus to Jesus. Zinzendorf led them to repent and repair relations. This process of reconciliation culminated in a united communion service in 1727. What happened next changed the course of history. A Moravian historian writes of the encounter:

> The Holy Ghost came upon us and in those days great signs and wonders took place in our midst. From that time scarcely a day passed but what we beheld His almighty workings amongst us. A great hunger after the Word of God took possession of us so that we had to have three services every day, 5:00 and 7:30 A.M. and 9:00 P.M. Everyone desired above everything else that the Holy Spirit might have full control. Self-love and self-will as well as all disobedience disappeared and an overwhelming flood of grace swept us all out into the great ocean of Divine Love.

What followed this powerful encounter with the Holy Spirit is known as the birth of the modern missions movement, as many Moravians gave their lives to take Christ to the nations of the world. The fuel for this movement was a prayer meeting that lasted twenty-four hours a day, seven days a week, for 100 years!

It has been said that prayer is the key to revival. But prayer alone is not the key. The kind of prayer that brings Heaven down is united prayer. And there is no united prayer without reconciliation. What would happen if we would lay down our differences in the Body of Christ and cry out to God in fervent, united prayer? Maybe the next great awakening would sweep through our cities. Maybe the next wave of missions would cover the earth with the glory of God. I long to be a voice of reconciliation in my city for the name, Jesus. How about you?

> Urged by love, to every nation
>
> Of the fallen human race
>
> We will publish Christ's salvation,
>
> And declare His blood-bought grace;
>
> To display Him, and portray Him,
>
> In His dying form and beauty,
>
> Be our aim and joyful duty.
>
> NICOLAUS ZINZENDORF

The story of Zinzendorf and the Moravians moves me to the core. It demonstrates what a life-changing encounter with God can do to a community of people, propelling them into fully realized purpose. They were gripped with the love of God and couldn't keep it to themselves. An insatiable desire for the glory of God rests on those who have been revived. A deep humility, quiet strength, and fervent love mark those who have genuinely been with Jesus. The more you are with Him, the more you look like Him, sound like Him, and think like Him. You carry the fragrance of Christ.

What would a revived Church look like? It would look like Jesus. And if anything can put the dragon on the run, it's Him. True revival routs the religious spirit like nothing else. The dragon's influence can't survive in that environment because it's too much like Heaven for his liking.

KINGDOM COME

The scholar George Eldon Ladd defined the Kingdom this way: "The Kingdom is primarily the dynamic reign or kingly rule of God, the sphere in which the rule is experienced." Make no mistake. God is on His throne. But the truth remains that this Kingdom of God is not currently experienced everywhere. Jesus said, "The Kingdom of Heaven is like yeast that a woman took and mixed into about sixty pounds of flour until it worked all through the dough." (Matthew 13:33 NIV) Much like the yeast in a batch of dough, the Church is to be the vehicle through which the Kingdom comes to Earth. So, if the Kingdom is the demonstration of the rule and reign of Jesus, then revival is an outbreak of that Kingdom. The Kingdom is the leaven that influences everything around it. But how can we be the conduit for Heaven's influence if another leaven has influenced us?

The leaven of the religious spirit has so infiltrated the Church that, in some respects, the Church looks nothing like it's supposed to look, acting in no way as a cultural change agent, bringing the reality of the Kingdom of God to every sphere of society. Instead, religion has majored in the minors, so the Bride is distracted.

The mission of Jesus has taken a backseat to things far less important. And the world carries on, broken, like God's heart, as we carry on with our schedules, church events, blogs, books, and Bible studies, with little to no regard for the people we're called to reach with the good news. The assignment goes unfulfilled. Eden remains a romantic idea of the past as we continue to climb the Tree of the Knowledge of Good and Evil, busy with everything except what Jesus asked us to do.

The greatest hindrance to the Church's fulfilling its assignment on Earth is the religious spirit that has infiltrated it. This is the reason I wrote this book. I see the glaring inadequacies of the modern Church.

I see it in myself. But I haven't written this book only to point out the disparities. I believe with all of my heart, and pray with all the faith I can muster, that the Church would return to its most authentic identity and assignment. It's not just a good idea. It must happen.

In recent years, I've had friends give up on the Church, and some have even left the Christian faith altogether. I've watched leaders and role models of the faith fall and fall hard, leaving a wake of destruction affecting thousands, even millions. I've watched the Church fall in love with politics, fighting for power and influence and abandoning the way of the Jesus they claim to love and follow.

In reality, the "Jesus" they love and follow is the version that agrees with their politics. So now we have a Republican Jesus, a Democratic Jesus, and any other kind of Jesus we care to create, just as long as it justifies how we think and act. All the while, a generation looks on and sees a version of the Church that repulses them.

For people who have trusted these church leaders yet have never firmly trusted Jesus, the fallout is not easy to overcome. In a time when many are deconstructing their faith and some even turning away from the Church, I think in most cases, those walking away do not have a problem with Jesus or His mission. Instead, they have seen the radical disparities between the mission of Jesus and the religiosity of the people who claim to know and follow Him. I am not discouraged by this. On the contrary, hope rises in me because I know that a pure, spotless Bride is emerging from the ashes of the post-Christian era, unscathed by the dragon's breath and ready to take her place at Jesus' side. And what a Bride she will be!

This Church will be made up of those who have seen His glory, know their identity, and are fulfilling the mission of their King. I believe the coming revival that is already stirring will be a revival of the heart of Jesus in the heart of the Church.

I can see it now. I see a praying Church, convinced of its calling, rising with new fire in its heart, renewed vision, and a manifesto on its lips:

No more dragons.

No more religious fog clouding our view of the great commission.

No more squabbling over secondary issues that distract us from the main thing.

No more pharisaical looking down our noses at those with whom we disagree.

No more exalting law over love, shutting the door on those who desperately need the gospel.

No more settling for belief without experience that validates its authenticity and demonstrates its veracity.

No more allegiance to cold traditions that have outlived their original truths.

No more avoidance over influence, preserving our dignity, unwilling to stoop to love the lowly.

No more high-minded doctrine taking the place of whole-hearted devotion.

No more control and manipulation.

No more friendly fire.

No more embracing offense.

No more fear of man.

This revolution starts with all of us taking our place in the Kingdom. It starts with me. It starts with you. So rise with courage, certainty, and strength. Let's take back what belongs to our King.

Let's kill the dragon!

ACKNOWLEDGMENTS

To my wife, Bethany,
I'm so grateful for your support and belief in me throughout the journey of writing this book. You have been the true hero by my side, slaying dragons with me as we faced the challenges and obstacles that come with ministry and raising a family together. You've always stoked the fire of my dreams and passions, always having the right words to keep me going. I can't believe I get to be your husband. I love you.

To Bailey, Reid, and Rebekah,
I'm incredibly proud of you guys and love being your daddy. You have taught me what unconditional love is all about. I pray this book helps you to love Jesus and others well for the rest of your lives.

I want to extend my deepest gratitude to my editor, Hope Myers, whose invaluable contribution and unwavering support played an integral role in bringing this book to fruition. As an editor, Hope's keen eye for detail, meticulous approach, and understanding of the message I wanted to convey elevated this book beyond my expectations. I am grateful for the countless hours she dedicated to meticulously combing through the manuscript, offering insightful suggestions, and helping to shape and refine it. I couldn't have done it without her!

I sincerely thank Matt Higgins, who brought my book to life. His ingenious and visually stunning cover design has exceeded all my expectations, capturing the book's essence within its artistic brilliance.

Special thanks to Theresa Harris, Jamie Moore, and Wes Pickering for encouraging me to write and being there to answer all my questions.

This book stands as a testament to the power of community. I am humbled and grateful to the extraordinary individuals who have been a source of inspiration and unwavering support throughout my journey. To my parents, friends, and mentors, your presence in my life has made all the difference, and I cannot express my appreciation enough.

BIBLIOGRAPHY

Associated Press (1992, May 30). Stigma that's still associated with leprosy has biblical roots that may be tied to mistranslation. Deseret News. https://www.deseret.com/1992/5/30/18986753/stigma-that-s-still-associated-with-leprosy-has-biblical-roots-that-may-be-tied-to-mistranslation.

Bailey, A. C. (2017). The Weeping Time: Memory and the Largest Slave Auction in American History. Cambridge University Press.

Calvin, J., & Bonnet, J. (1858). Letters of John Calvin: Compiled from the Original Manuscripts and Edited with Historical Notes. 33. Baker Book House.

Deere J. (2020). Why i am still surprised by the power of the spirit : discovering how god speaks and heals today. Zondervan.

The Editors of Encyclopaedia Britannica. (2023, June 2). Temple of Jerusalem | Description, History, & Significance. Encyclopedia Britannica. https://www.britannica.com/topic/Temple-of-Jerusalem.

Friedman, D. (2001). They Loved the Torah: What Yeshua's First Followers Really Thought about the Law. Messianic Jewish Publisher.

Gerhard Schrader: Father of the Nerve Agents. (n.d.). Collaborative for Health & Environment. https://www.healthandenvironment.org/environmental-health/social-context/history/gerhard-schrader-father-of-the-nerve-agents.

Goddard, R. (2022).Rocket Science for Beginners. The Attic. https://www.theattic.space/home-page-blogs/2022/6/16/rocket-science-for-beginners.

Good done by the church - Christianity. (n.d.). Christianity. https://www.christianity.org.uk/article/good-done-by-the-church.

Greenfield J. (1928). Power from on high; or the two hundredth anniversary of the great moravian revival 1727-1927.

Horn, A. (2018). Justin Martyr "Dialogue with Trypho." Horn.

Kelly, J. (2006). Early Christian Creeds. A&C Black.

Key Life, & Guzman, E. (2020, July 10). Brennan Manning on God's Love. Key Life. https://www.keylife.org/articles/brennan-manning-on-gods-love/.

Ladd, G. E. (1974). The Presence of the Future: The Eschatology of Biblical Realism. 109. Eerdmans.

Lyons, I. O. (2012). Against Heresies. CreateSpace.

NFL 100. (n.d.). NFL.com. https://www.nfl.com/100/originals/100-greatest/plays-54.

Rafferty, J. P. (n.d.). "Mr. Gorbachev, Tear Down This Wall!": Reagan's Berlin Speech. Encyclopedia Britannica. https://www.britannica.com/story/mr-gorbachev-tear-down-this-wall-reagans-berlin-speech.

Schaff, P. (1562). History of the Christian Church, Vol. VIII.

Schiffman, L. H. (2023, February 1). Building the second temple. My Jewish Learning. https://www.myjewishlearning.com/article/second-temple/.

Shelley, B. (2013). Church History in Plain Language: Fourth Edition. 186-191. Zondervan Academic.

Shelley, 206-207.

Shelley, 207-209.

Shelley, 224-233.

Shelley, 247-251.

Stephens, K. (2023, April 8). Opinion | 11 million, not 6 million, died in the Holocaust. The Washington Post. https://www.washingtonpost.com/opinions/11-million-not-6-million-died-in-the-holocaust/2017/05/26/6fdcc270-3f1c-11e7-b29f-f40ffced2ddb_story.html.

Storms, S. (2020). Understanding Spiritual Gifts: A Comprehensive Guide. Zondervan

Strasser, D, and Mullins, R. "Creed." Universal Music Publishing Group.

Streett, R. A. (2013). Heaven on Earth: Experiencing the Kingdom of God in the Here and Now. 240. Harvest House Publishers.

Tolkien, J.R.R. (2023). The Hobbit. Harper Collins UK.

Tozer, A. (2022). Going Higher with God in Prayer: Cultivating a Lifelong Dialogue. Baker Books.

United States Holocaust Memorial Museum (n.d.). Book Burning. Holocaust Encyclopedia. https://encyclopedia.ushmm.org/content/en/article/book-burning

Wesley, J. (1820). A Collection of Hymns: For the Use of the People Called Methodists.

Gunter Akridge is the founding pastor of The Dwelling Church in Savannah, Georgia. He calls coastal Georgia home, alongside his wife Bethany, and their three children. Gunter's primary calling lies in fostering spiritual renewal within the Church to ignite spiritual awakening throughout the broader culture. His dedication to this vision shapes his writing and teaching, and fuels his passion for creating transformative experiences through the written and spoken word.

www.ingramcontent.com/pod-product-compliance
Lightning Source LLC
Chambersburg PA
CBHW070702130626
46553CB00005B/1802